SOUTH

CAROLINA

KILLERS

SOUTH CAROLINA KILLERS

CRIMES OF PASSION

MARK R. JONES

Charleston   London

THE
History
PRESS

Published by The History Press
Charleston, SC 29403
www.historypress.net

Copyright © 2007 by Mark R. Jones
All rights reserved

Cover design by Marshall Hudson.

First published 2007

Manufactured in the United States

ISBN 978.1.59629.395.3

Library of Congress Cataloging-in-Publication Data

Jones, Mark R. (Mark Rowell), 1959-
South Carolina killers : crimes of passion / Mark Jones.
p. cm.
Includes bibliographical references.
ISBN-13: 978-1-59629-395-3 (alk. paper)
1. Murder--South Carolina--Case studies. 2. Murder victims--South
Carolina--Biography. 3. Capital punishment--South Carolina. I. Title.
HV6533.S6J65 2007
364.152'30922757--dc22
2007036997

Contents

Introduction

As Long As We Are Able

"We owe respect to the living; to the dead we owe only the truth."
—Voltaire

What you hold in your hand is a collection of murder stories in South Carolina that spans one hundred years—1903 to 2003. So, let's talk about murder.

I remember an old joke I learned in Sunday school. It went like this: How long did Cain hate his brother? Answer: As long as he was able.

Ever since Cain killed Abel in the Garden of Eden, humans have been horrified and fascinated with murder. And the first murder was a good one. The two brothers fought over God's rejection of Cain's sacrifice to the Lord, and His acceptance of Abel's. As they struggled, Abel, who was stronger, physically defeated Cain, and then mercifully spared his life. As soon as Abel turned his back, however, Cain attacked with a stone, killing his brother in cold blood.

That pretty much sums up the history of humanity and homicide. Humans have always killed one another, and other humans will always be curious to know about it. Look at all the books written about murder—from the Agatha Christie–styled genteel murders, to the gritty, hard-core, matter-of-fact killings in Andrew Vachss's gritty noir novels, to the gruesome icy detachment of Bret Eaton Ellis's *American Psycho*, to the thousands of true-crime nonfiction books, like *In Cold Blood*.

And then you get into television and motion pictures. It seems more than half the TV programs have always been crime oriented. Think of all the cop shows, from the methodical *Dragnet* to the more realistic *Hill Street Blues* and *CSI*. Then there are the courtroom heroics of *Perry Mason* and *Matlock*, and the world-weary private detective—take your pick from about twenty thousand of them: *Magnum P.I.*, *The Rockford Files*, *Mike Hammer*, etc.

The point is, homicide is hot. It always has been and always will be. The two most famous murder cases in American history happened 102 years apart—the 1892 murder of Andrew and Abby Borden, and the 1994 murder of Nicole Brown Simpson and Ronald Goldman. In both cases, the accused was related to the victims—Lizzie the daughter, and O.J., the ex-husband. The two cases have so transcended American culture that the accused murderers have entered that pantheon of celebrities known only by one name, probably because of their acquittal and the public perception that both Lizzie and O.J. got away with it.

One of the most interesting times in Southern history was the period after the War Between the States, called Reconstruction. Even if the original concept of Reconstruction was good, in application it was corrupt, violent and heavy-handed. Reconstruction laid the groundwork for the Jim Crow era in the South and created a legacy of bitterness that still manifests itself in many ways, such as low-quality public education and several generations of government-dependent citizens. It has also perpetuated a valley of racial division on both sides that is responsible for the caustic attitude of "if you disagree with me, you must be evil or racist." Not just a different opinion, but *evil!* Unfortunately, too many of the murder stories contained in this volume have a racist element at their core.

In 1993, the murder rate in the United States was 9.5 per 100,000. In Louisiana, it was 20.3. By contrast, in 1900, Edgefield County, South Carolina, had a murder rate of 30.5 per 100,000, a higher rate of carnage than medieval England. Two of the stories in this volume have their roots in Edgefield County.

There were some stories I obviously *had* to include, like the Susan Smith case that became a national tragedy and the sad story of George Stinney, age fourteen when he was executed by South Carolina. Other stories I chose for the most obvious reasons—they are interesting and serve as cautionary tales.

Some of the names of victims and family members have been changed for privacy purposes.

Until next time…

Chapter One

Murder in Broad Daylight (1903)

Political corruption is a common thread that runs throughout the history of mankind. At the beginning of the twentieth century, South Carolina did not take a back seat to anyone as far as corruption among politicians, as this story illustrates—the murder of a newspaper editor by the second highest elected official in South Carolina, who walked away a free man.

JANUARY 15, 1903. It was just after noon in Columbia, South Carolina, and the editor of the *State* newspaper, Narciso Gener Gonzales, was walking home for lunch. Gonzales was the son of General Ambrosio Jose Gonzales, a Cuban revolutionary general who opposed Spanish rule. His mother was Harriet Rutledge, the daughter of William Elliott, a wealthy South Carolina rice planter, state senator and writer.

N.G. Gonzales had gained national renown during the Spanish-American War. His coverage of the famous charge up San Juan Hill by Teddy Roosevelt and his Rough Riders helped cement that incident in the American psyche.

It was a cold, blustery day in Columbia, and Gonzales was walking with his head down against the cold wind. His shoulders were hunched and his hands were thrust deep in his coat pockets. As he turned the corner of Main and Gervais Streets, he met lame duck Lieutenant Governor Jim Tillman and two state senators on the sidewalk.

Tillman approached the editor and said, "Good morning. I got your message." He then pulled out a German Luger and shot Gonzales in the stomach.

A nearby policeman arrested Tillman. Gonzales was carried back to his office in the *State* building half a block away, and then to the hospital. The

Cuban editor lingered unconscious for several days, but contracted peritonitis (blood poisoning) from the gut shot that had ruptured his intestine.

JANUARY 19, 1903. N.G. Gonzales died and two days later, most of the businesses in Columbia closed in honor of the man who had started the *State* newspaper in opposition to the politics of his murderer's uncle, Governor Ben "Pitchfork" Tillman. Several hundred people braved a cold, rainy day to pay tribute to the fallen editor.

JANUARY 21, 1903. A coroner's inquest determined that Tillman had shot and murdered Gonzales, and a trial date was set for September. Tillman's jail cell was soon furnished with books, comfortable chairs and other accoutrements. Meanwhile, the powerful Tillman political machine began to maneuver and manipulate—anything to get the results they desired.

What could have led the lieutenant governor to gun down the most prominent newsman in the state in broad daylight? Gonzales and the Tillman family political machine had conducted a decade-long public feud, of which the shooting was just the climax of a series of slights, innuendoes and disagreements.

James "Jim" Tillman's political mentor was his Uncle Ben, the former South Carolina governor who was serving as a U.S. senator at the time of Gonzales's murder. The Tillman family had a colorful history.

Jim Tillman's grandfather had once killed a man during an argument. His uncle John was killed in a duel. Uncle Oliver was killed in a "domestic dispute." Uncle Thomas was killed in the Mexican-American War.

Jim's father, George Tillman, became an Edgefield lawyer and was elected to the state legislature and U.S. Congress. During one of his reelection campaigns, George was playing faro, a popular nineteenth-century card game, when he "inadvertently" shot and killed a bystander. Fearing prosecution, he fled to California, but later returned and was convicted of manslaughter. Despite the fact that he was in prison, George Tillman still practiced law from his well-decorated jail cell. He survived several duels, but one year before his son gunned down Gonzales, George was killed over a gambling dispute.

George's youngest brother, Benjamin R. Tillman, became a successful Edgefield County farmer and learned politics during Reconstruction. Ben hated two things: Republicans and blacks who were not subservient. Tillman became commander of the Sweetwater Saber Club and during the 1870s conducted a small-scale war against African Americans that included harassment and assault. He was involved in the execution of a black state senator, Simon Coker. Two of Tillman's men executed Coker with a shot to the head. Tillman ordered a second shot just in case he was "playing possum."

Ben Tillman helped elect General Wade Hampton in 1876 as part of the Red Shirts, who were so called because they rode around wearing white shirts stained with red to symbolize the blood of the black men they had killed. Ben Tillman believed that a reformed Republican was no better than a corrupt Republican—they were both guilty of trying to endow blacks, something Tillman could not accept. He worked hard to rid South Carolina of the Republican/Yankee rule with "a settled purpose to provoke a riot and teach the Negroes a lesson [by] having the whites demonstrate their superiority by killing as many of them as was justifiable."

Tillman began to attract statewide attention through his diatribes against blacks, bankers and aristocrats who he claimed were running and ruining the state. Ben Tillman believed that farmers were "butchering the land by renting to ignorant lazy Negroes." Gonzales was outraged by Tillman's speeches and behavior, and he began to write negative stories about the Tillman campaign.

APRIL 1890. Jim Tillman wrote an anonymous editorial in the *Fairfield News* complaining about the press coverage of his uncle's recent speech. The letter was signed "Fair Play" and had several disparaging references about the "sly and cunning nature" about Gonzales. Gonzales demanded to know the identity of "Fair Play."

NOVEMBER 1890. Despite having never held public office, Ben Tillman was elected governor with the stated goal to return white rule to South Carolina; anyone who opposed him deserved to be destroyed. He stated, "We do not intend to submit to Negro domination and all the Yankees from Cape Cod to hell can't make us submit to it…we of the South have never recognized the right of the Negro to govern white men, and we never will."

As blacks began to lose their tenuous grip on political power, violence against them increased. Lynching throughout the state became commonplace. Any white woman who accused a black man of rape was essentially giving him a death sentence. The *Newberry Herald* considered the rape of a white woman by a black man too serious to merit the niceties of a legal trial. Elizabeth Porcher Palmer wrote that she hoped lynching would "have a good effect."

During the 1890s, four members of the state's congressional delegation had committed murder. Pistols were considered part of a man's uniform—rich or poor, black or white—which lead a state judge to call South Carolina "an armed camp in a time of peace."

JANUARY 1891. N.G. Gonzales used his influence to blackball Jim Tillman from membership in the South Carolina Club. In a story published in the

Columbia Record, Gonzales claimed that "a man who would make a false and scurrilous attack upon a gentleman and HIDE BEHIND HIS INCOGNITO was not a fit person to become a member of the club."

Tillman challenged Gonzales to a duel. They were to meet on the traditional Savannah River sandbar. Dueling was illegal in both Georgia and South Carolina, but as the river was the border between the two states, gentlemen often met on this "no man's land" to duel. Tillman arrived in Augusta to meet Gonzales, who never appeared. Tillman sent Gonzales a bill for his hotel room charges.

An anti-Gonzales paper, the *Charleston World*, stated, "People who constantly carry chips on their shoulders now-a-days, get little credit from the world at large, and are liable, sooner or later, to run into a snag."

FEBRUARY 18, 1891. The first issue of the anti-Tillman newspaper the *State* was published under the editorial control of Gonzales, who believed that a paper "must hold opinions and voice them boldly."

1894. Ben Tillman ran for the U.S. Senate, and during the campaign he called President Grover Cleveland "an old bag of beef." Tillman was elected to the Senate by a large majority.

JANUARY 14, 1895. Meanwhile, Ben's nephew Jim Tillman was creating his own legacy of violence and corruption. He owed an Edgefield lawyer, Barnard Evans, an insurance payment, and when Tillman arrived at Evans's office, the two men got into an argument and drew pistols on each other. Tillman was grazed in the chin by a bullet and Evans was shot in the shoulder.

MARCH 1897. James William Thurmond, solicitor of Edgefield County, was part of the Tillman political machine. Thurmond, as a state legislator, had nominated Ben Tillman to the U.S. Senate and worked hard for his election. Next to the Tillman family, Thurmond was known as one of the most powerful men in Edgefield County, possibly because of his support of the Tillman regime. His son, J. Strom Thurmond, would become the most powerful man, not only in Edgefield County, but in South Carolina during the next fifty years.

As Will Thurmond walked out of the Edgefield courthouse to his law office down the crowded street, he was followed by Willie Harris, an avowed Tillman hater and devout reader of the *State*. One afternoon when Harris was in town, drunk and loitering outside the courthouse, looking for trouble, he had told a friend, "I've got a good knife and a Colt's pistol in my pocket."

Harris began to shout and curse at Thurmond, taunting him. Thurmond ignored the diatribe and continued walking until Harris called him a "low, dirty scoundrel." Thurmond pulled out a pistol and shot Harris in the chest, killing him instantly. Thurmond immediately turned to the nearest bystander and asked, "You can see it was self-defense, can't you?" During his trial for murder, Thurmond hired James Tillman to defend him. It took a jury thirty-five minutes to find Thurmond not guilty.

OCTOBER 1898. Jim Tillman joined the military during the Spanish-American War and rose to the rank of colonel.

JUNE 1900. Colonel James Tillman announced his candidacy for the lieutenant governor's office, in which he advocated the closing of all black schools. When his opponent, former Confederate officer John Sloan, boasted that he had not been shot during the war, although his horse had, Tillman responded, "Because you were hiding behind the horse."

OCTOBER 1900. The *State* published a story that Tillman had been arrested during the raid of a gambling den in Augusta, and that he had appeared in court the next day under an assumed name. Tillman claimed the stories were false, but offered no proof to the contrary.

When Tillman won the election, Gonzales, in an editorial written for the *State* noted, "Well, we can stand it if the Senate can."

MARCH 1901. The *State* reported that Tillman had been arrested and acquitted for racing in the streets of Edgefield, and three months later they claimed he lost $1,000 betting on a cockfight. Gonzales wrote, "We have no penchant for cockfighting and still less for the Hon. James H. Tillman."

1902. Lieutenant Governor Tillman helped raise money for a sword for local Rough Rider hero Major Micah Jenkins. President Teddy Roosevelt, leader of the Rough Riders during the Spanish-American War, was scheduled to visit the Charleston Expo, and agreed to perform the presentation ceremony.

However, in Washington, D.C., Senator Ben Tillman physically attacked the other South Carolina senator, John McLaurin, and the two men fought on the Senate floor. Tillman ended up with a busted nose and McLaurin had open wounds on his face. Tillman was officially censured by the Senate. President Roosevelt cancelled a dinner invitation to the White House that he had previously extended to Senator Tillman.

When Lieutenant Governor Tillman heard that the president had cancelled his uncle's dinner invitation, he promptly withdrew the president's invitation to the award ceremony. The *State* immediately attacked Tillman for "this act of boorishness," and Gonzales led the fundraising drive to purchase the sword.

MARCH 24, 1902. When the rumors that Jim Tillman was planning to run for governor became known, the headline on the front page of the *State* read, "JAMES H. TILLMAN PROVED A FALSIFIER." In the story, Gonzales called Jim Tillman "unworthy of public trust." The Gaffney *Ledger* commented that Tillman was "a falsifier, gambler, drunkard, blasphemer and defaulter."

JULY 23, 1902. The *Ledger* called Tillman "a gambler, a liar, and a drunkard." Tillman read the accusations to the crowd at a campaign appearance and then claimed only to be offended at being called a liar, because *that* was a lie, leaving the audience to assume that the rest of the story was true—he *was* a gambler and a drunkard.

Throughout the summer, the *State* published daily reports about Jim Tillman's character and behavior. He was called a "degenerate" and "the criminal candidate."

AUGUST 4, 1902. A rumor circulated that Lieutenant Governor Tillman had once, while in a drunken rage, dangled his infant daughter over an open well. The *State* published a cartoon that subtly implied the rumor was true.

AUGUST 25, 1902. The day before the primary election, Gonzales published a story claiming that "it was somebody's responsibility to stand forth and show his [Tillman's] falsity and depravity." The *State* claimed it was protecting South Carolina against "debauchery and dishonesty."

After his defeat, Jim Tillman wrote a letter asking the general election voters to support every candidate not endorsed by the *State*. He wrote, "But for the brutal, false and malicious newspaper attacks headed by N.G. Gonzales, I believe I would have been elected. Some day the people of South Carolina will believe that I am far, very far, from being the man I have been painted."

Tillman offered to resign as Lieutenant Governor if Gonzales would call him "a liar, a blackguard, and a coward" to his face.

JANUARY 15, 1903. Tillman gunned down Gonzales. He pleaded "not guilty," claimed self-defense and was denied bail. Tillman's law partners got the trial moved from Richland County to Lexington County, a Tillman political stronghold. They also succeeded in getting the case assigned to Judge Martin B. Gary, the nephew of Frank Gary, a longtime associate of the Tillman political machine.

The solicitor assigned to prosecute the case was none other than James William Thurmond, whom Tillman had successfully defended for a self-defense shooting five years before.

SEPTEMBER 28, 1903. Tillman's trial opened in Lexington, South Carolina. The prosecution provided witnesses to establish the fact that Gonzales did not walk around armed, and that the editorials the accused found offensive were echoes of the same writing from other newspapers.

More than six hours' worth of *State* editorials were read into the record by Tillman's defense lawyers in an attempt to prove the shooting was justified.

The atmosphere around the courthouse was tense, on the precipice of mob violence. Ewan Justice, a reporter from Texas, was amazed by the spectacle. He wrote, "Practically everyone here connected with either side of the case is armed. Some men carry two pistols, while others are content with one. These guns are of large caliber, and make witnesses look as if they had an umbrella under their coats."

OCTOBER 14, 1903. The jury had the case for twenty hours before word came down that they had arrived at a decision. Several hundred Tillman supporters rushed to fill the courtroom. The better marksmen took the best positions in case there was an uprising by the outraged losing side when the verdict was announced. This indicates that the Tillman people knew the outcome *before* the jury made their announcement. This is not surprising, since the entire case had been weighted toward the Tillman side—location, judge and prosecutor were favorable toward the Tillmans. There were also rampant rumors that several of the jury members were longtime Tillman family supporters.

Few people were surprised when the jury announced Tillman not guilty.

OCTOBER 16, 1903. The *State* headline read, "JAS. H. TILLMAN ACQUITTED OF THE CHARGE OF MURDER." A sub-headline claimed "the cards were stacked." The paper called the trial and verdict "a farce."

The *New York World* stated that if any editor who criticized a public official could be killed without fear of punishment, then the verdict signaled "the death of the free press in the Palmetto State." South Carolina was now "a barbarous commonwealth, a disgrace to American civilization."

DECEMBER 12, 1905. N.G. Gonzales was memorialized with an obelisk erected at the corner of Senate and Sumter Streets in Columbia.

APRIL 2, 1911. The *State* published a brief obituary on page one, column three, which read, "Asheville, NC. James H. Tillman, at one time lieutenant governor of South Carolina, died here tonight."

The Gonzales Obelisk in Columbia, South Carolina, which was erected in honor of the murdered newspaper editor. *Photo by Joel R. Jones.*

Chapter Two

Last Man Hanged
The Execution of Daniel Duncan (1911)

Was Daniel Duncan "murdered" by the state of South Carolina by official execution? The truth may never be known.

JUNE 21, 1910. Around 9:30 a.m., Charles Karesh, a shoe dealer at 546 King Street in Charleston, noticed a man loitering outside his store, holding a stick. The man seemed to be looking through the window next door at Max Lubelsky's tailor shop.

Karesh stepped out onto the street and asked, "What are you doing out here?" The black man then entered Lubelsky's store without replying. Karesh walked back inside his own shop. Karesh later described the man as "a round-faced Negro…about five feet and six inches tall…clean shaven and wore a blue serge suit of clothes." He appeared to "be between 25 and 30 years old. I would know him again if I saw him."

Frank Cross, a black driver for Bahr's Express, stepped into Lubelsky's just after 11:00 a.m. He had a package to deliver to Lubelsky that had arrived the previous day on the steamer. When Cross walked in, there was "a colored man standing inside the store." Cross asked the man to get Mr. Lubelsky to come and sign the delivery book. The mysterious man told Cross that Lubelsky had gone across the street. The black man claimed Lubelsky had just hired him as the porter, and he had been left in charge while Lubelsky was out of the shop.

Cross waited a few minutes for Lubelsky. During that time, Cross claimed that the porter put on a "blue sack jacket." He later said the man had a "round face, was clean-shaven straight and narrow and about 28 or 30 years of age. I would know this man if I saw him again," he claimed.

After fifteen minutes, Cross told the porter he would return later in the day to get his delivery book signed.

Sometime around 11:30 a.m., Mr. Posner (56 Line Street) walked into Lubelsky's shop with his little girl. Mr. Lubelsky was not inside the store, so Posner walked to the rear, thinking Lubelsky might be feeding the chickens he kept in the backyard. When the search of the yard yielded no sign of the tailor, Posner sat his daughter down on a stool and leaned over the counter. Lubelsky's body was lying beneath the counter with a pool of blood under his head and shoulders.

Posner rushed around the counter and tried to talk to Lubelsky. When the shopkeeper did not respond, Posner rushed next door to Karesh's shoe shop. The police were notified. Both Posner and Karesh tried to communicate with Lubelsky. Karesh attempted to pick up Lubelsky, but the man only moaned and moved his hands. He never spoke.

Sergeant Stender was standing at the corner of King and Mary Streets when a street peddler hollered at him that Lubelsky had been killed in his store. Stender ran over to the store and found Lubelsky lying unconscious on the floor in a pool of blood. A quick search of the tailor's shop revealed a money drawer in the back room. There was no money in the drawer, but a few coins and checks were scattered about the floor. The left front window display had been forced open, and it appeared that someone had removed a suit of clothes. The rest of the store showed signs of being quickly searched. Stender also found a stick lying on the floor beside Lubelsky.

Detective Clarence Levy was walking down the street and noticed a crowd gathered at the intersection of King and Reid Streets. Levy entered the store and quickly took charge of the investigation. Lubelsky was taken in a police ambulance to Roper Hospital, where he died within the hour. His wife and daughter were in New York visiting her brother at the time of the attack. Telegrams were sent to notify them of Lubelsky's death.

For the next two weeks, the police were baffled. They interviewed witnesses and arrested a few people on suspicion, but all to no avail. And then came a bizarre turn of events.

JULY 7, 1910. Headline from the *News and Courier*: "LUBELSKY'S WIDOW ATTACKED."

Mrs. Lubelsky was in the store about 10:40 a.m. when a young black man entered. While he was in the process of purchasing some clothing, a fourteen-year-old black boy, Jos Middleton, entered. The other customer backed away and encouraged the teenager to conduct his business. When Middleton had left the store, Mrs. Lubelsky resumed wrapping the clothes for the first customer. When she reached out her hand for the eight-dollar payment, the man hit her.

"I saw him raise his hand about so high," said Mrs. Lubelsky, indicating a position above her head, "and then I didn't know anything more." She staggered out into the street screaming for help.

Two men across the street, Issac Goodman and Moses Needle, heard the woman's screams and looked in that direction. They noticed a black man walk casually out of the Lubelsky store and turn south on King Street. Goodman and Needle ran after the man, who made no attempt to flee until the two men were almost upon him. He then darted into a Chinese laundry six doors down from Lubelsky's. Goodman and Needle apprehended the man in the laundry and held him until Officer Stanley arrived.

Mrs. Lubelsky was taken to her home above the store. Dr. Pearlstine was called and dressed the woman's wound.

Stanley put the attacker under arrest, and he was placed in the patrol wagon. When asked his name, he replied, "Daniel Duncan, sir." A crowd of men, women and children had gathered around the paddy wagon. One man reached through the bars and punched Duncan in the back of his head. The wagon quickly left for the police station.

Chief Boyle wanted to have Mrs. Lubelsky identify her assailant, so he ordered the wagon driven back to the scene. When the paddy wagon arrived, she came downstairs and identified Duncan as her assailant.

Police immediately went to Duncan's home at 48 Vanderhorst Street, where they discovered a vast amount of new clothes and jewelry, for which they could find no explanation. They interviewed dozens of witnesses and accumulated physical evidence.

JULY 8, 1910. Chief Boyle formally entered two charges against Daniel Duncan. The first was assault and battery with intent to kill against Mrs. Lubelsky, and the second was murder against Max Lubelsky. Duncan was committed to the county jail on Magazine Street awaiting trial in the next term of the Court of General Sessions.

The Old Charleston Jail still stands at 17 Magazine Street, a monument of a time when law enforcement was less nuanced, more forceful and often cruel. It was built in 1802 at four stories, with an octagonal tower. A more foreboding structure does not exist in the city. When Duncan was imprisoned, it had no running water or electricity and was rampant with overcrowding and poor sanitation.

A typical description of a prisoner was:

> *A forlorn, dejected creature, his face…so completely matted with dirt and Made fiendish by the tufts of hair that hung over his forehead…He had no shoes on his feet, and a pair of ragged pantaloons and the shreds of a striped*

Old Charleston City Jail, circa 1802. It is still standing in the center of the city, and by all accounts, is one of the most haunted structures in South Carolina. Photo by author.

shirt without sleeves, secured around the waist with a string...In truth he had scarce enough on to cover his nakedness and that so filthy and swarming with vermin, that he kept his shoulders and hands busily employed.

Grand juries often complained to the sheriff that conditions in the jail were intolerable and must improve, but law officials never heeded the warning.

One of the most imposing sights in the jail yard was the gallows, visible to all prisoners on death watch. The method of hanging used at the jail was different than what most people imagine, where the condemned climbs up stairs and is dropped from a platform. In the Charleston jail yard, the condemned stood on the ground with the noose around his neck. The one-inch-thick rope was suspended from a twenty-foot post and ran through a pulley at top. The other end of the rope was attached to a five-hundred-pound counterweight that was dropped, yanking the condemned into the air and snapping his neck for a quick death.

OCTOBER 7, 1910. Duncan went to trial for the murder of Max Lubelsky. He had already been convicted of assault and battery against Mrs. Lubelsky, even though he pleaded not guilty. He was convicted mainly from Mrs. Lubelsky's identification of him as her assailant, as well as fourteen-year-old Jos Middleton's identification.

As Duncan was being led into court for the murder trial, Mrs. Lubelsky jumped from her seat and hollered at him, "You killed my husband! Why didn't you kill me?" She was removed from the courtroom.

OCTOBER 8, 1910. It took the jury less than two hours to find Duncan guilty of the murder of Max Lubelsky. During the sentencing phase of the trial, Duncan testified that he had worked the night shift at Geilfuss's bakery for thirteen years, and was engaged to have been married on July 13, six days before the attack on Mrs. Lubelsky.

He stated that on the morning of her attack, he was walking on King Street across from the store when he heard a woman screaming. He looked up in time to see a woman running out of Lubelsky's shop. He said he was apprehended by a group of white men, beaten and accused of assaulting Mrs. Lubelsky. He denied being in the Chinese laundry. He also denied ever being in the Lubelsky store.

The jury sentenced him to execution by hanging.

JULY 6, 1911. During an interview with a reporter from the *Charleston Evening Post*, Duncan lay in his hammock, which had a view of the gallows, and declared his innocence. He said, "When a man makes up his mind to undergo a thing, he can do it, if he has faith. I am a member of the church now, and feel that I will meet my Maker tomorrow. I go to Him with a clear conscience, and often I have thought that I would be glad when the day came, for I believe that my soul will be saved."

JULY 7, 1911. On the day of his execution, Duncan spent his last hours with six African American ministers. The night before, he had written a statement.

> *Gentlemen: How can you have the heart to stand to see the advantage taken of a poor man for nothing? But anyhow that will be all right. I leave it between you and the Lord. He knows all. Tell Mr. Cross who went down to the court house and kiss the Bible and say that I was the man he saw in the shop, which he know was a lie. But tell him that is all right. We will meet one of these days, and we will talk the story over. I ain't got no evil in my heart for him. I ask the Lord to forgive him, and have mercy on*

him, because I want him to meet me in heaven, because I know that I am saved. I feel like a changed man. I was praying for this day to come so I can see my Lord and my mother. She is waiting to receive me in the Kingdom, because I know that she is there. She is preparing a place for me.

I must congratulate Capt. Hanley. Ever since I were in here, he sure did treat me fine. Anything I want and I ask him for, he will be sure to let me have it, therefore I ask the Lord to help him, that I may meet him in heaven. Also Capt. Rice. He sure treat me like a gentleman. Also Mr. Strobel. I hope I will meet them in heaven. I know I that I am going there to rest. My dear father did all he can for his dear son. He could not do any more. I am well pleased with him for what he has done for me. Therefore I am going to prepare a place for him to meet me and my dear mother, also my sisters and my dear brother. Tell them that I am at rest, because I am innocent, and the Lord knows that I am today. It is nothing but dead advantage taken of me, for something that I don't know nothing about. But anyhow, that will be all right. I will meet you when the roll is called.

The only people officially attending the execution were jail officials, about twenty police officers and Duncan's minister, the Reverend L.R. Nichols of Morris Brown Methodist Church. However, hundreds of people showed up. According to the *Charleston Evening Post*, "Roofs in the neighborhood of the jail were crowded with spectators, and the streets running by the jail were thronged."

At half a minute past 11:00 a.m., Duncan stood on the ground below the gallows, hands and legs tied, with the rope around his neck and black mask pulled over his head. Seconds before the counterweight was dropped, Duncan fainted and his unconscious body was snatched into the air and then dropped quickly. His head twisted right and after a few leg spasms, the body dangled. Thirty-nine minutes later, he was pronounced dead and removed from the gallows. He was buried in Morris Brown Cemetery.

Duncan wrote a letter to his pastor before his death that in part read, "My Dear Pastor: On the day which is my last day, I can not tell a lie. But anyhow, that will be all right. I will be brave and take it like a man. It is only one time to die."

Daniel Duncan was the last man to be executed by hanging in South Carolina. The next execution was in the electric chair. For Duncan, it may have been only "one time to die," but it possibly may have been the wrong time to die. All the evidence that convicted Duncan was circumstantial. The last man hanged in South Carolina may have been innocent.

Chapter Three

The Perfect Murder of an SOB (1933)

A Charleston socialite who was known as a wicked gossip was mysteriously shot in the city's most exclusive neighborhood. Her murder was never solved, but five years later a series of tornadoes tore up the historic city and revealed a long hidden clue.

NOVEMBER 1, 1933. It was a typical night for Charleston—warm, with a slight breeze; most people would have described it as balmy. Elsa Eberhand was driving on Meeting Street south of Broad Street, the neighborhood of the bluebloods, filled with colonial and antebellum mansions, many handed down for several generations. Those who were not lucky enough to live in this high-toned area called the residents SOBs, an impolite, yet usually accurate acronym for South of Broad.

As Elsa drove in the descending dusk past the corner of Meeting and Water Streets, she noticed what appeared to be a body lying on the sidewalk. Elsa sped up and drove as quickly as possible to a nearby store. Johnny Townsend, a sophomore at the College of Charleston, was working that evening. Elsa described what she had seen and asked for his help. He got into her car and they returned two blocks to the intersection.

Johnny jumped out of the car and ran over to the body lying facedown on the sidewalk. Johnny turned the body over. "Why, it's Mrs. Ravenel!" he exclaimed. Almost everyone in town knew Mrs. Mary Ravenel, the widow of John Ravenel, who owned two mansions in the neighborhood.

Mrs. Ravenel began to moan and babble, and Johnny realized that she was injured. He picked up her purse and they carried her to the car and drove her to Roper Hospital. Mary Ravenel was conscious when they arrived. A nurse asked Mary who her doctor was and the injured woman was able to give his name. The nurse went to place a call for the doctor while an attendant asked her questions.

The intersection of Meeting and Water Streets, where Mrs. Ravenel was found injured. *Photo by author.*

"What happened to you?"

"A man hit me," Mrs. Ravenel replied.

"Was he driving an automobile?"

"I don't know."

Because she was coherent and showed no visible wound, the hospital staff guessed she had been struck by a car. They left her alone, resting on a bed. The nurse returned and said that Mrs. Ravenel's doctor could not be located. Did she have another physician they could call? She gave them the name of two others. The nurse finally located one of the doctors on the phone. She told the physician not to rush, as it was not an emergency.

During that time, Mary Ravenel died.

A hospital doctor examined her body and initially concluded she had been stabbed. A car from the funeral home arrived, and her body was taken to prepare for burial. As the mortician examined her body, he discovered a bullet wound in Mrs. Ravenel's arm. She had been shot.

Dr. Kenneth Lynch, professor of pathology at the Medical College of South Carolina, was summoned to perform an autopsy. Lynch discovered the bullet had gone cleanly through the forearm and pierced Mrs. Ravenel's heart. The bullet was a copper-jacketed, .38-caliber, which was uncommon. Lynch also suspected it had been hand-filled. No powder burns were found, and Lynch could not determine from what distance the shot had been fired. There had been almost no external bleeding. Mrs. Ravenel had died of internal hemorrhaging. Her body was bruised, leading Lynch to surmise she had dragged her body a few feet before collapsing face down on the sidewalk.

The police arrived at the scene of the crime. A crowd had gathered, and the residents were questioned. Someone claimed to have heard a gunshot at a quarter to ten. Someone else had heard a cat crying. Another claimed to have heard a woman scream and a car drive away. Others heard footsteps of someone running. That was the sum of their evidence. There was no weapon at the scene, no eyewitnesses and no physical evidence. Mrs. Ravenel's purse had been found at the scene and nothing seemed to be missing. The jewelry she was wearing was not stolen. The police were puzzled.

Why would someone want to kill Mrs. John Ravenel?

She was the former Miss Mary Mack of Detroit. In the 1890s, she had married William Martin, owner of several plantations near Savannah, Georgia. Martin died in 1903, leaving Mary with four children to raise. Three years later she married John Ravenel of Charleston. It was quite a step up for Mary. The Ravenels were one of the true blueblood families of South Carolina. The first Ravenel arrived in Charles Towne in 1681.

John and Mary lived at 5 East Battery, an 1849 mansion that contained twenty-four rooms and six baths. The most spectacular feature of the house was the triple piazza that commanded a grand view of Charleston Harbor. John's father, St. Julien Ravenel, had studied medicine in France and owned the Stony Landing plantation. During the War Between the States, St. Julien had helped design the *Little David*, a semi-submersible boat that was the forerunner of the modern-day submarine. He had also developed the first limestone mining works in the state at Stony Landing. Mary had married not only into money, but also into the upper crust of Charleston society.

After John's death, Mary moved to the smaller, but older, Ravenel house at 12 Tradd Street (circa 1780). She entertained often, was active in church and volunteered within the community. She enjoyed a weekly game of bridge, and often dined at the restaurant of the Fort Sumter Hotel at 1 King Street. She was a loyal friend to many, but she had one weakness: she was a wicked gossip. Her tongue was tart and she delighted in wagging about the people of Charleston, secure as she was in her position in Charleston society. She relished the gossip about the latest indiscretions, whose son had flunked out of college and whose daughter had to suddenly "go to Europe for nine months." She loved to speculate about so-and-so's son who had never married, but lived with the same man for ten years!

One of Mary's favorite gossip targets was Mr. Paine, "that effeminate man, the photographer," she called him. Paine lived at the corner of Price's Alley and Meeting Street. Mary gossiped about him so much that it was an open secret of how much Paine despised her. But there was little he could do but complain to his friends about her annoying prittle-prattle. He was a mere photographer, one of the "little people," and she was a member of the most exclusive club in South Carolina—a Charleston SOB.

The police were puzzled at Mary's shooting and soon were at a dead end. All they had were theories. Some detectives believed the killer had been shooting at cats and accidentally shot Mrs. Ravenel. Others thought it was robbery and the criminal had been interrupted before he could make away with her jewels and purse. Very few people thought her death was intentional.

NOVEMBER 27, 1933. Robert Cox was questioned. He was a nineteen-year-old Charleston man who lived at 42 Vanderhorst Street. He had confessed to two holdups of nearby stores, but denied any connection with the murder of Mrs. Ravenel. He was released and never charged with her murder.

Mayor Maybank offered a reward of $250 for "information leading to the apprehension and conviction of the person or persons responsible for the death." The reward went unclaimed.

Five years passed, and during that time the Charleston police examined every pistol confiscated with every crime committed in the city, but none matched the weapon that had been used to shoot Mrs. Ravenel. They never found a match for a .38-caliber, copper-jacketed, hand-filled bullet.

During the next few years, Mr. Paine, the object of Mrs. Ravenel's once hateful gossip, died of natural causes.

SEPTEMBER 29, 1938. Mother Nature took a hand in solving the murder. That Thursday morning, the city was covered by forbidding, low-hanging clouds. At about 8:00 a.m., a tornado touched down on James Island. At about the same time, some men standing in front of a filling station watched a black waterspout twist its way across the Ashley River toward the peninsula. As the twister passed the bridge toward them, it picked up a truck and dumped it on the ground. In less than a minute, the roof of the filling station had been ripped off the building.

A second funnel hit the city. All the windows of city hall were blown out and the old Confederate Home on Broad Street was severely damaged. St. Michael's Church received a hole in the roof. Another twister smashed onto Meeting Street, snaking its way between King and Water Streets and Price's Alley. The Fort Sumter Hotel was battered and wrecked, as was the Carolina Yacht Club. By 8:30 a.m., all was quiet. During that half hour, dozens of automobiles had been overturned and some were tossed through store windows. More than two hundred people were injured and thirty-two were killed.

However, the oddest result from the "Day of the Tornadoes" may have been what was discovered in a shattered house on Price's Alley, the previous home of the photographer Mr. Paine. As a salvage crew sorted through the shattered remains of the house, they discovered a filing cabinet fallen over on its side, with a hole punched in the wall. Under the cabinet, halfway out of the wall, lay a gun. The gun was turned over to the police. A bullet was found in the chamber—a copper-jacketed, hand-filled, .38-caliber bullet that matched the bullet that had been found in Mary Ravenel's body.

The murder of Mrs. John Ravenel officially remains unsolved.

Chapter Four

Hip Pocket Justice in Edgefield
The Execution of Sue Logue (1941)

Murder, sex, revenge, family feuds, political maneuvering…this story has everything, including in the last paragraph one of the greatest bits of political scandal in South Carolina history. It's so outrageous it has to be true!

APRIL 9, 1923. The *Augusta Chronicle* wrote, "The old state of South Carolina, with a population of less than a quarter of that of the six New England states, in 1890 reported nearly three times their number of homicides."

Edgefield County, on the western South Carolina border close to Augusta, Georgia, was home to a lot of those murders. In 1816, Parson Weems called it "a very District of Devils." During the period of 1933 through 1938, Edgefield County had one of the highest murder rates in South Carolina, but also the lowest conviction rate. Judge T.S. Sease commented, "Too many people are getting off and justice is being thwarted."

It was a rural place, dominated by sharecroppers, close-to-the-land farmers and independent bootleggers. Despite Prohibition, liquor was, according to the Edgefield *Advertiser* on March 7, 1923, "as plentiful as water, you can't step out of your door without smelling whiskey or seeing someone drunk." Violence was not a stranger to most. Almost every man was armed, and hip pocket justice was a common occurrence. Most families had a history of violence. The first story that leads off this collection, "Murder in Broad Daylight," illustrates some of that attitude—the rampaging Tillman family and James William Thurmond's murder of Mr. Harris and subsequent acquittal.

1900. Sue Bell Stidham was four years old when her father shot and killed a man. He was acquitted of murder, claiming self defense.

MARCH 1914. Sue Stidham married Wallace Logue. Wallace and his brother George operated a large successful farm that included cotton, corn, wheat, cattle, sheep, hogs, chickens and a sawmill. Like many Edgefield families of the day, the Logues had their own storied history of violence.

1924. Sue Bell Logue began teaching in Edgefield County School. At that time, the teachers had no requirement of a high school diploma. In 1930, the law changed and Sue was no longer qualified to teach. Two petitions were passed around the county—one in support of hiring Sue (circulated by the Logue family), and another that was against her hiring. When Sue presented her petition to Davis Timmerman at his store, he refused to sign it. He told her he was trying to "remain neutral." However, Superintendent of Education J. Strom Thurmond supported Sue, as did one of the school's trustees, her brother-in-law, George Logue. She was hired.

Why would a woman who did not meet the qualifications be hired as a teacher? According to the book *Strom: The Complicated Personal and Political Life of Strom Thurmond* by Jack Bass and Marilyn Robinson,

> *The stories still whispered in Edgefield tell of Strom's long affair with Sue, who campaigned for him when he ran for county superintendent of education and whom he allowed to teach in the county schools despite unwritten rules generally excluding married women from teaching positions. Her reputation for sexual prowess was such that men told stories of her reputed vaginal muscular dexterity. The lore includes a tale of her and Strom found flagrante delicto in the superintendent's office.*

None of that was difficult to believe, because this *was* the Strom Thurmond who campaigned as a segregationist while conducting a sexual affair with a black woman, which resulted in an illegitimate child. This was the Strom who in the 1950s put the moves on Washington, D.C. writer Sally Quinn *and* her mother at the same reception. This was the Strom who, at age sixty-six, would marry a twenty-two-year-old Miss South Carolina and begin to have children with his young wife, which prompted Senator John Tower of Texas to remark, "When he dies, they'll have to beat his pecker down with a baseball bat in order to close the coffin lid!"

There was also speculation that Sue was sleeping with her brother-in-law George as well. The Logue brothers ran their farm as a partnership—Wallace was the "man in the field," whereas George handled the managerial duties. It seemed Wallace was always at work, away from the house, while George always seemed to be *at* the house. On many occasions, it was George who attended social functions with Sue, rather than Wallace. George took Sue shopping in Augusta. Many in town thought George and Sue were husband and wife.

SEPTEMBER 26, 1924. Joe Frank Logue Sr. was killed by his brother-in-law, Cliff Owdom. Cliff claimed he had been attacked by his drunken brother-in-law and shot him twice in self-defense. Using the testimony of a black man, Willie Jones, Owdom was acquitted for murder. Wallace and George Logue publicly stated their intention to "get even" with Jones for helping the murderer of their brother go free.

Wallace, Sue and George Logue became the de facto parental figures for Joe Frank Jr., who was seventeen at the time of his father's murder.

DECEMBER 17, 1925. Hugh Cogburn, husband of Maude Logue, was found bludgeoned to death in his car. His murder was never solved.

JUNE 12, 1927. Willie Jones, "under the influence of whiskey," disrupted church services at the Willow Springs Baptist Church. A deacon contacted the local magistrate, W.S. Logue, who arrived with his two sons, Wallace and George. Jones pulled a pistol, and the Logue brothers instantly gunned him down in the church—one shot to the head, another to the hip. The brothers were acquitted of murder by self-defense. Two of the jury members were Fred Dorn, a sharecropper for the Logues, and Davis Timmerman, their neighbor.

NOVEMBER 1930. Sue got pregnant, which jeopardized her position as schoolteacher. She asked Dr. A.R. Richardson for an abortion. Abortion was illegal in South Carolina, and the doctor refused to perform the operation. Several days later, Dr. Richardson was summoned to the Logue house because Sue was ill. He discovered she was ill due to a botched abortion and was suffering from an infection. He treated her and issued a death certificate for the child, listing "premature birth" as the cause. The gossip was hot around town that the baby's father had been George, not Wallace.

A few years later there was an incident on a school bus. Sue was riding behind the driver and one of Sue's students, Mary Timmerman, was being harassed, groped and fondled by a group of boys. Sue did nothing to help the girl, which incensed Mary's father, Davis Timmerman.

Davis Timmerman told a reporter from the Augusta *Herald* that he had once found Sue Logue in a "compromising position" with a neighbor.

DECEMBER 1938. Joe Frank Logue Jr., who was seventeen when his father was killed by his uncle, became a policeman on the Spartanburg force.

Joe Frank quickly got a reputation as an energetic officer. He joined the vice squad and took an FBI fingerprint identification class. He was voted Spartanburg's "Most Outstanding Policeman."

JUNE 1939. Sue was not hired as a teacher that year, and she did not hide her anger at those she deemed responsible—John Bryan; Ivy Claxton; the principal, who claimed she received threats from the Logue family for not supporting Sue; but most of all, Davis Timmerman.

APRIL 10, 1940. Clarence Gillam, an African American, was shot in the face by Fred Dorn, who was white. Dorn, a sharecropper for George and Wallace Logue, did not like "niggers" to drive by his home. Gillam was the brother-in-law of O.W. Phillips, who worked for the Timmerman family. The bad blood between the Timmerman and Logue families seemed to be escalating. Dorn's children would often holler out "nigger" when O.W. and Clarence passed the Dorn house. Dorn also had accused the men of "stirring a neighbor's hogs."

JULY 8, 1940. Dorn was tried for the murder of Clarence Gillam and acquitted within fifteen minutes by self-defense.

AUGUST 1940. Wallace and George Logue stopped Davis Timmerman one day on the bridge that crossed Turkey Creek and threatened to drown him. Davis Timmerman was running for office, and later that month during voting Sue confronted Timmerman at the polling place. In front of a crowd of witnesses, Sue threatened to kill Timmerman.

SEPTEMBER 1940. A mule owned by Davis Timmerman broke through a fence that bordered the Logue farm. The mule kicked a cow that later had to be put down. Timmerman and Wallace Logue agreed on the cost of the cow. Timmerman told Logue to stop by the store to pick up his money.

SEPTEMBER 30, 1940. Wallace Logue stopped at the Timmerman store, which served the rural community as a gas station/grocery and hardware store. When Timmerman handed over the agreed-upon amount of money, Logue demanded more. Timmerman refused, and Wallace Logue picked up an axe handle from a display and attacked Timmerman. Davis was able to ward off the blows long enough to grab his pistol next to the cash drawer. He shot Wallace Logue three times—through the arm, the chest and in the head.

When Timmerman realized Logue was dead, he walked next door to the house and told his wife what had happened. He closed the store and left to get the sheriff.

OCTOBER 1, 1940. As Wallace Logue's funeral procession traveled past the Timmerman house on South Carolina Highway 43, Davis Timmerman sat on his front porch and watched. Many in the Logue family thought it disrespectful that Timmerman did not have the grace to stand when the procession passed. Joe Frank Jr. was sitting in a car with his mother and brother Wallace. When he saw Timmerman sitting on the porch, Joe Frank said, "I'm gonna kill that son of a bitch!"

MARCH 2–3, 1941. Davis Timmerman was acquitted of the charge of murder at an Edgefield trial by self-defense.

A few days later, Carrie Gillam, the mother of Clarence who had been killed by Fred Dorn and who did the laundry for the Timmermans, was walking across the pasture from the Timmerman house to her home. Carrie noticed Fred Dorn lying in the grass in the pasture with his gun. Fred got off the ground and pretended to be hunting. Carrie assumed he had been lying in wait for Davis Timmerman.

It became a daily event for the Logue truck to drive up to the front door of the Timmerman store, with George driving, Sue next to him and Fred Dorn standing in the truck bed with a rifle. The truck would stop and Dorn would point the rifle at the door of the store. When a customer asked about the Logues' behavior, Timmerman said, "They do that every day."

During a trip to Spartanburg, Sue Logue told her nephew, Joe Frank Jr., that she wanted him to find a man to kill Davis Timmerman, and that she and George were willing to pay $500.

JULY 1941. Joe Frank Jr. knew a man in Spartanburg named Clarence Bagwell, who had served three years for a manslaughter conviction. One day, Joe Frank said to Bagwell, "Clarence, some parties want you to bump a fellow off. Will you do it for them? I will tell them more about it later."

"All right," Bagwell replied.

A week later, Joe Frank asked if Bagwell was ready to do the job.

"What's in it for me?" Bagwell asked.

"My people will pay you $500."

"I'll kill *everybody* in Spartanburg County for $500," Bagwell said. "And me as broke as I am. I'm ready to go at any time."

AUGUST 1941. Joe Frank took a two-week vacation and saw George and Sue almost every day. He told them he had "found a man."

SEPTEMBER 1941. Joe Frank brought Bagwell to Edgefield County. On the evening of their arrival, they parked in front of Timmerman's store. "That's where the dirty rat stays that killed my uncle," Joe Frank said. He then described Davis Timmerman to Bagwell.

Joe Frank also made arrangements with Howard Cannon, who was a salesman at the Pierce Motor Company in Spartanburg, to borrow a car. Cannon told Joe Frank that the cars on the lot did not carry insurance, but he was welcome to borrow his own car, a 1941 Deluxe Tudor Ford, for the trip.

SEPTEMBER 17, 1941. Joe Frank picked up Bagwell in the Deluxe three miles out of Spartanburg about 2:30 p.m. The car contained two pistols, a raincoat and a quart of Canadian Club whiskey. During the ninety-mile drive to Edgefield, the men drank whiskey from the bottle. By the time they reached Timmerman's store, Joe Frank was "under the influence of whiskey very much," according to Bagwell. He later admitted they were both "highly intoxicated." Joe Frank got in the back seat and covered himself with the coat. Bagwell drove up to the store and noticed a car with some black men in it. There was also a white man in the store who soon departed. "We might as well get it over with," Bagwell told Joe Frank Logue.

Bagwell entered the store and approached Timmerman, who was behind the counter. He asked for chewing gum and three packs of cigarettes. When Timmerman reached for the cigarettes, Bagwell pulled out the gun and "I began to pull the trigger. I emptied the pistol which held six cartridges because I heard it snap the last time I pulled the trigger." As he ran to the car, Bagwell noticed a lady and little girl across the street who began to holler and scream.

Bagwell jumped in the car and sped away. He and Joe Frank finished the quart of liquor on the drive back to Spartanburg and arrived home around 9:30 p.m.

SEPTEMBER 22, 1941. Joe Frank gave Bagwell $500 and the two men drove to Lake Lanier on the North Carolina–South Carolina border. They dismantled the gun and tossed the pieces in different parts of the lake.

NOVEMBER 5, 1941. O.J. Brady, chief detective of Spartanburg County, received a mysterious phone call. The female caller asked Brady, "Do you know about a man who was killed in a store in a county in the lower part of the state?" Brady checked around and learned about the Timmerman murder.

The next day, Brady met with the anonymous caller, a woman, who told Brady that someone named Clarence Bagwell had made $500 for killing somebody. She also told him that a local Spartanburg policeman was involved. She claimed Bagwell had come into her business and made a purchase, flashing a roll of money. When she asked how he got the money, he said "for killing Mr. Timmerman."

NOVEMBER 9, 1941. Bagwell confessed and implicated Joe Frank Logue Jr. When confronted, Joe Frank denied any involvement. He was arrested and put in jail. However, when his brothers Tom and Wallace visited him in jail, they asked, "Why did you do such a thing?" Joe Frank answered, "Because I thought I could get away with it."

NOVEMBER 10, 1941. A coroner's jury inquest recommended that Bagwell and Joe Frank be held for murder.

NOVEMBER 15, 1941. Joe Frank finally decided to sign a confession. He admitted to hiring Bagwell to kill Timmerman. He also implicated his Uncle George and Aunt Sue Logue. He claimed that they pestered him until he agreed to hire someone for the murder. Sheriff W.D. "Wad" Allen received little satisfaction from the confession, since George's mother, Anna "Mama" Logue, was his first cousin, making George Logue his second cousin.

NOVEMBER 16, 1941. Early that Sunday morning, Deputy "Doc" Clark arrived at the Logue home and asked George and Sue to meet him at the sheriff's office at 10:00 a.m. Within an hour, several Logue family members arrived at the house for support.

Before noon, George sent word to Sheriff Wad Allen that they could not leave the house because Mama Logue was ill. Sheriff Allen and Deputy Clark decided to drive out to the Logue house. They were met in the yard by George and Sue. The two cousins, George and Sheriff Allen, chatted for a moment, and then Allen entered the house to pay a courtesy call on Mama Logue.

While Allen and Sue were talking with Mama Logue, George walked out to his pickup truck and returned with his .410 shotgun. Deputy Doc Clark followed George, who placed the gun in his bedroom. While this was going on, Fred Dorn arrived at the Logue house.

George asked the sheriff, "Have you come for me and Sue?"

Allen responded, "Yes, I have, George."

Sue asked, "What have we done?"

The sheriff handed Sue the arrest warrant. George and Sue took a few minutes to read the document.

Mama Logue said, "Oh Wad, you are going to take all I've got."

George asked if he and Sue could have the chance to change their clothes, and Sheriff Allen agreed. George went to his room to change. Doc

Clark and Allen walked out of Mama Logue's room and waited in the dining room.

A moment later, George came out of the bedroom with a pistol and opened fire. His first shot hit Allen in the face, killing him instantly. Doc Clark yanked out his gun, but George turned and fired another shot, hitting the deputy in the stomach. Clark managed to fire back three times, hitting George twice—once in the arm and once in his side.

Fred Dorn appeared in the doorway from George's room and opened fire with the .410 shotgun. Clark's arm was shredded by the shotgun blast, but he still managed to turn and shoot Dorn. The bullet struck Dorn's spine, paralyzing him. Clark's pistol was empty, and he had been shot twice in the arm and stomach, yet he managed to approach George and knock him in the head with the butt of his gun.

Sue rushed out of Mama Logue's bedroom and slammed a chair down over Clark's head. He staggered outside and collapsed in the dirt. He reloaded his pistol and began to stagger down the dirt road, away from the house, looking for help.

Johnny Cogburn had learned that Sunday morning that his grandmother, Mama Logue, was ill and decided to visit. It was just before noon when he turned into the driveway of the Logue house and was greeted with the sight of the bleeding, staggering Deputy Doc Clark, waving a pistol. Clark ordered Johnny to drive him into town for help.

"They've killed Wad Allen," Doc Clark told Johnny. "You'll have to hurry; I'm bleeding to death on the inside."

Johnny drove ninety miles an hour to town. Church was just getting out when Johnny's car screeched to a stop in downtown Edgefield. Within a matter of minutes, the news of the shooting had spread. Clark was sent by car to the Augusta hospital.

J. Strom Thurmond, judge for the Eleventh Judicial Circuit, was coming out of church services at First Baptist when he heard the news that Sheriff Allen had been killed at the Logue home. With the sheriff dead and the deputy on the way to the hospital, Thurmond realized there was no other law enforcement officer in the county to take charge of this volatile situation. Because of his personal relationship with Sue and his standing in the community and influence as a judge, he hoped his presence would have a calming effect on everyone involved. Thurmond hopped in his car and headed to the Logue house.

By that time, law enforcement had begun to respond. Half a dozen officers, sheriff deputies and state troopers were on their way to the Logue house. Coroner Hollingsworth and Doctors Dunovant and Nicholson arrived at the house with three ambulances.

George Logue was taken to the hospital in Columbia; Dorn was taken to a Greenwood hospital and Sheriff Allen's body was removed.

When Judge Thurmond arrived around 1:00 p.m., a large crowd had already gathered. Dozens of cars lined the driveway to the Logue house. He noticed several people in the crowd were carrying guns. Sheriff Allen was a much-loved man by the locals, and Thurmond was concerned that more trouble could happen. There were several police officers around, just standing in the yard. They told the judge that Sue did not want to see anyone.

Thurmond approached the house. Someone inside hollered, "Don't come in, Strom. Or we'll have to kill you."

Thurmond removed his jacket, rolled up his shirt sleeves, turned out his pants pockets and opened his vest to show he was not carrying a gun. He was met at the front door by a man carrying a shotgun. "Sue don't want to see nobody," the man told Thurmond.

"I am Judge Thurmond! You put that gun down and tell Sue that I want to see her, right now!"

Thurmond was allowed to come inside and finally convinced Sue to leave, for her own safety. On the ride to the jail, she was finally served the warrant for conspiracy to murder. She told the officer, "Not guilty."

Fred Dorn died later that night in the hospital.

NOVEMBER 18, 1941. Deputy Clark died in an Augusta hospital of massive internal bleeding and organ damage.

JANUARY 21–26, 1942. George Logue, Sue Logue and Clarence Bagwell were put on trial in Lexington, South Carolina. Bagwell was found guilty of murder. George and Sue were found guilty of accessory before the fact of murder. Under South Carolina law, both crimes carried a mandatory death sentence by electrocution. George and Sue both claimed they were innocent and that they had no knowledge of Joe Frank's plan to hire Bagwell.

NOVEMBER 1942–JANUARY 1943. South Carolina Supreme Court and U.S. Supreme Court denied requests for a re-hearing. Governor Jefferies denied clemency.

JANUARY 15, 1943. Sue Logue, George Logue and Clarence Bagwell were executed, in that order. Sue cried when her long black hair was shaved from her head. Sue became the first woman in South Carolina to sit in "Old Sparky."

JULY 13–14, 1943. Joe Frank Logue Jr. was convicted of accessory before and after the fact of murder and sentenced to die in the chair.

FEBRUARY 25, 1944. Governor Olin Johnston commuted Joe Frank's sentence to life imprisonment.

DECEMBER 15, 1960. Joe Frank was paroled after serving nineteen years and died in 1990.

Judge J. Strom Thurmond went on active military duty in April 1942, but he was on leave at the time of Sue's execution. He rode with Sue from the women's penitentiary to the death house in Columbia. The driver of the van was Randall Johnson, a black man who worked for the state as a driver and messenger for officials. When Thurmond was elected governor in 1946, Johnson became one of Strom's most trusted drivers. Thurmond was elected to the U.S. Senate from South Carolina in 1954, and upon his retirement in 2003 he was the longest serving senator in American history, a total of forty-eight years. He died on June 26, 2003, and was buried at the Edgefield Cemetery.

According to driver Randall Johnson, on the afternoon of January 15, 1943, on their way to the death house, Thurmond and Sue were in the back of the van "a-huggin' and a-kissin' the whole day." Joe Frank Jr. later said that his Aunt Sue was "the only person seduced on the way to the electric chair."

Chapter Five

Too Young To Die
The Execution of George Stinney Jr. (1944)

This is the sad saga of the youngest person ever executed in the United States. It was the inspiration for the 1989 Edgar Award–winning book for Best First Novel, Carolina Skeletons, *by David Stout. The book became the basis for the 1992 movie of the same name starring Lou Gossett Jr. and Bruce Dern.*

1944. For such a small town, Alcolu, South Carolina, can claim to be the home of some notable Americans. Althea Gibson, the first African American woman to play tennis at Wimbledon, and Peggy Parish, author of the famous Amelia Bedelia children's books, were both born in the town. Alcolu can also boast to being the birthplace of five South Carolina governors. Most of the residents, black and white, worked at the Alderman Lumber Company Mill, farmed or both.

In 1944, most people in the tiny mill town were just trying to get by and hoping the few local boys who were serving in the war would make it back home. The most recent American casualty totals for World War II had just been released—19,499 killed, 45,545 wounded, 26,339 missing and 26,754 captured. Every day the newspaper was filled with death tolls and descriptions of war horrors, and though no one knew it, the worst was yet to come. The D-Day invasion of Normandy was two and a half months away.

MARCH 24, 1944. Betty June Binnicker, age eleven, and Mary Emma Thames, age eight, went to pick flowers that afternoon. Betty June asked permission to take a pair of scissors and then told her family, "We'll be back in about thirty minutes." The girls rode off together on one bicycle. No one was concerned. The girls often played on this side of town, and several people saw the familiar scene of the two girls riding double.

Right: Cover of the Edgar Award–winning novel *Carolina Skeletons*, based on the events of Alcolu murders and George Stinney's execution.

Below: Neighborhood in Alcolu, South Carolina. *Photo by author.*

They passed by the Stinney house. Even though the Stinneys were black, both girls knew the Stinney kids. Katherine Stinney and her older brother, George Jr., were in the front yard. "We're looking for maypops," Betty June said. "Do you know where they are?"

Katherine told them no, and the two girls rode off on their bike.

When the two girls didn't return by dark, the Binnicker family was panicked. Soon a town-wide search was launched, with hundreds of volunteers. They searched through the entire night. About 7:30 a.m. the next morning, some men found several small footprints in the soft ground and followed the footprints along a narrow path on the edge of town, where they found the pair of scissors lying in the grass nearby. Following the path with more urgency, the searchers discovered a large ditch filled with muddy water. They could see the outline of a bicycle beneath the murky surface. Scott Lowden jumped into the water, and the bodies of the two girls were dragged out. Both girls had severe head wounds—Mary Emma's skull was fractured in five different places and the back of Betty June's skull was smashed.

Within a few hours, local sheriff's deputies arrested George Stinney Jr. His youngest sister, Katherine Stinney Robinson, later recalled, "And all I remember is the people coming to our house and taking my brother. And no police officers with hats or anything—these were men in suits or whatever that came. I don't know how they knew to come to that house and pick up my brother."

George was taken to the sheriff's office, where he was interrogated. In 1944, there were no Miranda rights to be read to the accused. George was locked in a room with several white officers. Neither of George's parents were allowed to see him. Within an hour, Deputy H.S. Newman announced that Stinney had confessed to the murders. Stinney told police that he wanted to have sex with Betty June, but the only way to get her alone was to get rid of Mary Emma. But Betty June fought him, so he killed her too. Stinney then led the police to the scene, where they found a fourteen-inch-long railroad spike. Deputy Newman wrote a statement on March 26, 1944, and described the events.

> *I was notified that the bodies had been found. I went down to where the bodies were at. I found Mary Emma she was rite [sic] at the edge of the ditch with four or five wounds on her head, on the other side of the ditch the Binnicker girl, were [sic] laying there with 4 or 5 wounds in her head, the bicycle which the little girls had were beside of the little Binnicker girl. By information I received I arrested a boy by the name of George Stinney, he then made a confession and told me where a piece of iron about 15 inches long were, he said he put it in a ditch about 6 feet from the bicycle which was lying in the ditch.*

The town was horrified by the crime and overwhelmed with grief. Both girls' parents worked at the Alderman Lumber Mill, as did Mr. George Stinney Sr. Within a few hours, the grief among the millworkers had quickly transformed into a seething anger.

MARCH 26, 1944. About forty angry white men headed for the Clarendon County Jail and demanded mob justice, but sheriff's deputies were one step ahead of the folks. They had moved Stinney fifty miles away to Columbia.

B.G. Alderman, owner of Alderman's Lumber Mill, fired George's father. The Stinney family lived in such fear for their lives that they moved from town in the middle of the night, abandoning their son to his fate.

George Stinney Jr. was fourteen years, five months old when he went on trial. The first recorded execution of a juvenile in America was Thomas Graungery, age sixteen, of Plymouth Rock, Massachusetts, who was hanged for bestiality. On March 14, 1794, two young slave girls, "Bett, age 12" and "Dean, age 14," were executed for starting a fire that burned down a portion of Albany, New York. In 1988, the U.S. Supreme Court passed a ruling that "prohibits the death penalty for juvenile offenders whose crimes were committed before they were 16." Prior to 1988, there was no age limit for executions.

Lorraine Binniker Bailey was Betty June's older sister. She recalled that "everybody knew that he done it—even before they had the trial they knew he done it. But, I don't think they had too much of a trial."

Katherine Stinney Robinson later recalled, "I remember my mother cried so. She cried her little eyes all swollen. I would hear her praying. She said, 'I just want you to change the minds of men. Because my son didn't do this.' But it wasn't long after that that they just did it. He was gone."

The court appointed thirty-year-old Charles Plowden as George's attorney. Plowden had political aspirations, and the trial was a high-wire act for him. His dilemma was how to provide enough defense so that he could not be accused of incompetence, but not be so passionate that he would anger the local whites who may one day vote for him.

APRIL 24, 1944. More than 1,500 people crammed into the Clarendon County Courthouse. Jury selection began at 10:00 a.m. and was finished just after noon. The jury contained twelve white men. Due to the nature of the crime and the passion of the community, it certainly would have been in George Stinney's favor to have a change in venue. But defense attorney Plowden made no motion.

After a lunch break, the case was heard before Judge Stoll. Plowden did not cross-examine any of the prosecuting witnesses. His defense consisted of claiming that Stinney was too young to be held responsible for the crimes by law. In response, the prosecution presented Stinney's birth certificate stating that he was born on October 21, 1959, which made him fourteen years and five months old. Under South Carolina law in 1944, an adult was anyone over the age of fourteen.

The case had begun at 2:30 p.m. and closing arguments were finished by 4:30. The jury retired just before 5:00 p.m. and deliberated for ten minutes. They returned with the verdict "guilty, with no recommendation for mercy." The case took less than three hours to decide. Judge Stoll sentenced Stinney to die in the electric chair at the Central Correctional Institute in Columbia.

When asked about an appeal, Defense Attorney Plowden stated that there was nothing to appeal and the Stinney family had no money to pay for a continuance of the case.

Several local churches, in conjunction with the NAACP, appealed to Governor Olin D. Johnston to stop the execution. The governor's office received letters for mercy. Most cited Stinney's age as the mitigating factor why the execution should be dropped. One message was as direct as could be in 1944 by stating "child execution is only for Hitler." The Tobacco Worker's Union, the National Maritime Union and the White and Negro Ministerial Unions of Charleston asked Governor Johnston to commute the sentence to life imprisonment.

However, there were just as many, if not more, in favor of the execution who encouraged the governor to be strong. One of the more blunt letters to the governor stated, "Sure glad to hear of your decision regarding the nigger Stinney."

The governor decided to do nothing. He let the execution proceed.

JUNE 16, 1944. At 7:30 p.m., George Stinney Jr. was fitted into the electric chair. It had been designed for grown men, not children. He was five feet, one inch tall and weighed ninety pounds. The guards had a hard time strapping him into the seat. The mask over his face did not fit properly. When the switch was thrown, the force of the electricity jerked the too-large mask from his face, and for the final four minutes of his life, the spectators in the gallery had a full view of Stinney's horrified face as he was executed.

Stinney's sister, Katherine Stinney Robinson, was interviewed on the fiftieth anniversary of her brother's execution and said, "He was like my idol, you know. He was very smart in school, very artistic. He could draw all kinds of things. We had a good family. Small house, but there was a lot of love. It took my mother a long time to get over it. And maybe she never got over it."

The time span of the entire episode, from the girls' death to Stinney's execution, was eighty-one days.

Chapter Six

Perry Deveaux (1975)

A brutal rape and murder of a schoolteacher was finally solved by a persistent (and creative) cop and a motivated solicitor. Perhaps the oddest part of this story is that while he was in prison, Deveaux married a woman whose son became a serial rapist and killer whose crimes are covered in the companion volume Palmetto Predators: Monsters Among Us.

1975. Perry Deveaux was a seventeen-year-old African American of limited intelligence. He lived in Mount Pleasant at his grandmother's house on Venning Road, and worked on a garbage truck that covered the Sullivan's Island/Isle of Palms area of Charleston County. Close to his grandmother's house, there was a horse stable on Rifle Range Road where Perry had cleaned stalls for extra money for several years. Many of the riders knew him by name and would often spend a few minutes talking to the young man. One of the regular riders was twenty-three-year-old Kathleen Sanderlin of Sullivan's Island, a fifth grade teacher at Harbor View Elementary School on James Island.

NOVEMBER 28, 1975. Kathleen mounted her horse, cantered out for a ride in the countryside and never returned.

Perry had been drinking early that day, and he continued to drink as he mucked out stalls. Mid-afternoon, he walked to Gold's grocery story and purchased a quart of Budweiser and guzzled it straight down. That was when he saw Kathleen riding past. He met her on the riding path and greeted her. He then jumped in front of the horse, startling the animal. Perry grabbed Kathleen's arm and jerked her out of the saddle. She crumpled to the ground and Perry was on her immediately, flashing his knife. Kathleen began to scream.

"Shut up! Shut up!" Perry yelled, stabbing her each time he shouted, each swing of the blade slashing through her clothes and into her body. "Shut up! Shut up!" One of his swings slashed her throat and severed her vocal cords. The screaming stopped. Perry then used the knife to slice off her clothes, and then her panties. He dropped his pants and raped her while she was bleeding and choking on her own blood that was seeping into her throat. When he was finished he stood up, pulled up his pants and threw the knife away as far into the woods as possible. He ran away, not knowing if she was dead or alive, and not caring one way or the other.

Kathleen's horse returned to the stable empty. Someone went out to look for her, expecting to find her injured from being thrown, maybe slowly limping her way back to the stables. Instead, the searcher found her ravaged body lying in a dense undergrowth of brush along Four Mile road, a dirt road. Her body was rushed to the Medical University of South Carolina and pronounced dead on arrival. She had died from a severed artery in her abdomen.

Eugene Frazier had joined the Charleston County Police Department (CCPD) in the mid-1960s, in a time when racism was rampant in the department. Through hard work Frazier, an African American, rose through the ranks and after twelve years became a detective. Due to the years he spent as a patrolman, Frazier knew many of the people in the Mount Pleasant area. So when he was called to investigate Kathleen's murder, he immediately thought of Perry Deveaux, mainly because Frazier remembered Perry's often stated goal—"I'm gonna get me a white woman."

Detective Frazier and Corporal Curt Parsley went to Deveaux's grandmother's house. Accompanying them was the captain of detectives for CCPD. The captain was a racist with the attitude that a black detective was not capable of doing the job correctly. Since this was the vicious murder of a white woman, the captain of detectives decided he needed to take charge.

When they arrived at the house and Perry's grandmother opened the door, the cops could see Perry lurking in the dim background inside the house. Even in the gloom, Frazier immediately noticed the fresh scratch marks on Perry's hands and arms. While Frazier and Parsley watched, the captain harassed and humiliated the old woman, calling her stupid, and referred to Perry as "lazy and shiftless."

Frazier quietly asked the captain to take Perry into custody, but the captain told Frazier to mind his own business. The old woman was so alarmed by the captain's behavior that she closed and locked the door, and called a former prosecutor who was then a private defense attorney.

Perry was taken into custody, but with his lawyer in attendance. Perry denied any involvement with the murder and there was not enough hard evidence to charge him, so he was released. Frazier, however, was so convinced that Perry was guilty that he put a plan into action. He convinced Ronald Heyward, one of his informants, to get a job on the sanitation department with Perry. Heyward began to befriend Perry, with the goal of getting the young man to incriminate himself. When the captain discovered what Frazier was doing, he pulled the detective off the case. Local residents raised $5,000 for a reward, which grew in time to $15,000, for information that would lead to the discovery of Kathleen's murderer.

NOVEMBER 1981. Charlie Condon was elected to the Ninth Circuit solicitor's office, and during his first weeks in office, he looked at the files of unsolved murders. When he saw Frazier's name on the Kathleen Sanderlin case file, Condon called the detective into his office.

"Can this murder be solved?" he asked Frazier.

"Yes sir, if I work on special assignment out of your office and have no interference from the Charleston County Police," Frazier said.

Condon got Frazier assigned to the solicitor's office. Frazier's first move was to contact Ronald Heyward, who renewed his relationship with Perry Deveaux. The two men became friends. Perry was looking for a role model, an older man to teach him how to be a tough guy, and Heyward fit the bill perfectly. They became drinking buddies. Heyward reeled Perry in with a carefully constructed tale. He claimed that he had been involved in a killing in Chicago and now a local pimp and drug dealer wanted him to kill a prostitute. But he needed someone to help him; could Perry handle it?

Absolutely, Perry said. Heyward said they would have to meet with the pimp before the murder.

Then Frazier set the trap. Detective Rollo Brown was recruited to play the pimp. Brown had a full head of Jeri curls and dressed with gold chains and a flashy gold watch. He looked like the Hollywood stereotype image of a pimp.

JUNE 9, 1981. Heyward and Perry arrived at a hotel room. The pimp, Brown, was in the room, along with several black and white women posing as prostitutes. Brown sent the women away and turned to Perry. "My man here told me you wanted to do this thing. How do I know you're trustworthy? How do I know you got what it takes to kill a woman? Anybody can talk big."

Perry was so eager to prove his worth that he them gave a detailed description of his murder of Kathleen Sanderlin. Perry gave them several details not known to the public—like the fact that her pubic hair was a different shade from the brown hair on her head.

"You stick her? Where at?" Brown asked.

"I stick her here first," Perry said, slashing across his throat.

"In the throat?"

"Uh-huh, where she couldn't scream no more. Then right back around. I stick her in the navel part, then after I do it, I turned her around like this here and stick the back part."

Brown acted like he was impressed and told Perry, "I think you'll be good." They then discussed the details of the proposed murder of the prostitute.

Perry said, "Before I kill her, I want to f—— her."

Brown told him, "Do whatever you want, man."

Perry agreed to meet Brown again in a couple of days to get his advance money for the murder. Two days later, Perry Deveaux was arrested for murder and released on bond.

JANUARY 22, 1981. The court ordered the Department of Mental Retardation to examine Deveaux to determine whether he was competent to stand trial.

Perry's attorneys were worried that if he faced trial he would be convicted and receive a death penalty, so they asked for plea bargain. Perry would plead guilty in exchange for a life sentence. On the day of his sentencing, Perry arrived at the courthouse drunk. The judge had to postpone the hearing until later that afternoon for Perry to sober up.

MARCH 1, 1982. Perry entered Lieber Correctional Institute and would be eligible for parole in ten years.

While in prison, he struck up a friendship with Tess Evonitz. Tess was working as a phone operator in the prison when she met Perry. During slow times, many of the operators would chat with bored prisoners. Perry told Tess that, despite his confession, he was innocent. He claimed that the police had kept him under interrogation for hours and that, tired and defeated, he had confessed to a crime he did not commit. Tess believed him. She knew about his low IQ and she also knew about the unfairness of the prosecution of black-on-white crimes. She was convinced Perry was innocent.

Tess knew that developing an emotional attachment to a black man in prison, convicted of the murder of a white woman, was a stupid thing. But desperate women make bad choices. She saw this relationship with Perry as a way out of her brutal marriage to Joe Evonitz. She soon divorced her husband and married Perry.

Mug shot of Perry Deveaux. *Courtesy of the South Carolina Department of Corrections.*

JUNE 27, 2002. Tess's son, Marc Evonitz, committed suicide in Sarasota, Florida, after a high-speed chase with police. It was discovered Marc had kidnapped, raped and murdered six girls in Virginia and South Carolina. (For more on Marc Evonitz, read *Palmetto Predators: Monsters Among Us* by the same author.)

On the day before his stepson committed suicide, Perry Deveaux made his ninth appearance before the parole board. He was denied.

Chapter Seven

A Deadly New Year's Resolution (1992)

What is amazing about this story is how little public attention it got. That does not mean the crime was not horrific; it just wasn't noteworthy for the media. No one should die as Missy did.

D ECEMBER 29–30, 1992. Missy McLauchlin, twenty-five, had a history of drug problems. She had moved from Wixom, Michigan, to North Charleston, South Carolina, where she was living with her fiancé's family.

On the night she was murdered, she got into an argument with her fiancé, John Owen, at a nightclub. Angry and drunk, she marched out of the club and began to weave her way home on foot. Police spotted her and gave her a ride. But after the officers left, she set out on foot to walk to another club.

Three black men, Matthew Mack, Matthew Williams and Joseph Gardner, pulled up alongside in a car and started a conversation with the woman. They offered her drugs if she would come back to their trailer and have sex with them. Missy, impaired and angry, accepted their offer.

The three men had spent most of the day drinking and watching pornographic interracial videos with their girlfriends. At one point, Mack got angry at his white girlfriend and shouted that he wanted to "stab her," but that "any white would do." Williams chimed in, saying he wanted "to f—— a white woman."

Two hours later, the group watched a television news account of the biggest news stories of 1992. When the videotaped beating and arrest of Rodney King appeared on the air, the third man, Gardner, said that blacks "had endured four hundred years of oppression." He made a New Year's resolution to "kill a white bitch."

Later that night they went out for a drive and picked up Missy. They brought her back to the trailer where they lived. Even though they offered

Missy no drugs, she willingly had sex with them—at first. She started to resist when they tried to sodomize her. They held her down and took turns raping her.

During this time, Edna Williams and Indira Simmons, the girlfriends of Mack and Williams, were in the den of the trailer, watching television. They did nothing to help Missy.

Meanwhile, the men had put the word out around the trailer park that they had "captured a white woman." Three more men, sailors stationed at the Charleston Naval Base, arrived to take their turns raping Missy. After several hours, the men were satiated. The sailors left. Mack, Williams and Gardner decided to try to get rid of the evidence. They carried Missy to the bathtub and soaked her in bleach and hydrogen peroxide, using a nylon brush to scrub her skin. They even scrubbed out her vagina with bleach and peroxide.

While they were washing her, they discussed ways to kill her. They handcuffed and blindfolded Missy. Then they covered her with a coat and carried her to a car, forcing her down onto the back seat floorboard. They drove for a few minutes out of town. Missy managed to get out of the handcuffs and began to scream and struggle. Joseph Gardner, sitting in the front passenger seat, reached over the seat, grabbed her by the hair and jerked her head up and shot her twice in the face. They pulled over on U.S. Highway 78 fourteen miles outside Charleston. Gardner shot her four more times—three times in the face and once in the arm. They dumped her on the side of the road, drove back to Charleston and went nightclubbing for the rest of the evening. A passing driver found Missy, who was miraculously still alive. However, she died before the ambulance arrived.

It took authorities four days to identify her body. The next day they located the trailer where Missy had been raped and suspected a racial motive immediately. Inside the trailer they found a "crudely written racial diatribe" in the trailer, with racial epithets about white oppression, which claimed blacks were "justified in seeking revenge."

Racial tension in Charleston is always bubbling beneath the surface. As the largest slave port in colonial America, Charleston was a city dominated by the black population, but ruled by the iron fist of the minority whites. By 1800, Charleston had a black population of 11,000 and a white population of 8,800. As the first state to secede from the Union in 1860, and responsible for firing the first shot of the War Between the States, South Carolina—and Charleston in particular—was the most ardent defender of the "peculiar institution" called slavery. Two hundred years of repression do not disappear quickly, and sometimes not at all, especially when there are some who use the issue for personal and political purposes.

North Charleston Police Captain Charles Caldwell explained, "I think we have to be responsible to the community and the people we protect. I didn't want to believe this was a racial crime. And we tried to look for other motivations."

Local African American state Senator Robert Ford, taking a page from the Al Sharpton/Jesse Jackson play book, claimed Missy's murder was not motivated by race, but rather the *police* "should be investigated for inventing a racist plot." As outrageous as Ford's claim may look on the surface, the North Charleston Police Department in the 1990s did have some questionable racist arrests and incidents. Ford claimed that if the victim had been a black woman, the police would not have looked much harder for the real killers. Ford derided "decent white people" for remaining silent against white racism.

Letters poured into the editor of the Charleston *Post and Courier*. Many complained about the obvious double standard—that if the races had been reversed, the murder would have been national news, complete with protests, candlelight vigils and civil rights marches and visits by Al Sharpton and Jesse Jackson.

JANUARY 9, 1993. Police arrested seven people—Matthew Mack, Matthew Williams, the three sailors and the two women, Edna Williams and Indira Simmons, who were charged with being accessories to murder and sexual assault. Joseph Gardner, the man who had carried out his New Year's resolution to "kill a white bitch," could not be found.

Authorities learned that Gardner was AWOL from the navy and the FBI put him on the Ten Most Wanted list. Matthew Mack and Matthew Williams were convicted of kidnapping, rape and murder and given life sentences.

OCTOBER 20, 1994. Someone living in Philadelphia saw Joseph Gardner's picture in the post office and recognized him as someone who lived in the neighborhood. Gardner was arrested and brought back to Charleston for trial.

DECEMBER 1995. Gardner was convicted and sentenced to death.

MARCH 1999. The U.S. Supreme Court turned aside without comment an appeal by Gardner. Gardner had argued that his trial should have been moved elsewhere because of intense pretrial publicity.

APRIL 5, 2005. Gardner was granted a stay of execution by U.S. District Judge Henry Herlon so he could pursue federal appeals. As of this writing, Gardner is still on death row awaiting justice. Mack and Williams are available for parole in 2014.

Mug shot of Joseph Gardner. *Courtesy of the South Carolina Department of Corrections.*

Mug shot of Matthew Mack. *Courtesy of the South Carolina Department of Corrections.*

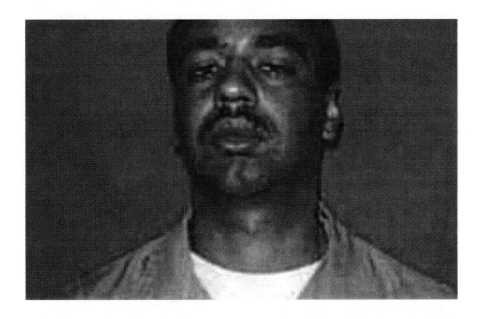

Mug shot of Matthew Williams. *Courtesy of the South Carolina Department of Corrections.*

Chapter Eight

The Murder of Rosemary Franco (1994)

As tragic as it is, in some neighborhoods a murder is almost commonplace. Take the preceding story of Missy. North Charleston was listed as the tenth most dangerous city in America in 2005. In that atmosphere, a violent crime is often just another incident. Every murder should be a sad and tragic event, not just a statistic.
This brutal murder shocked the upscale Ansonborough neighborhood in historic Charleston. Rosemary's murder remains officially unsolved, even though most officials involved in the investigation will tell you they know who the murderer was—they just couldn't prove it.

MAY 1963. Rosemary was born in Pittsburgh and adopted by Mildred and William Tomosky. She graduated from Syracuse University in 1985 with a degree in film studies and moved to New York to work in the movie business. To make ends meet, she got a job as a restaurant hostess on the side. She found herself drawn into the food industry and enrolled at the International Pastry Arts Center. She earned her degree and began to work with master chef Albert Kumin, who had been chef at the White House during the Carter administration.

She met Sergio Franco, a graduate of the French Culinary Institute, and in 1987 the two were married. They worked in various New York restaurants until 1991. Sergio was mugged and began talking about leaving New York because it "wasn't safe." Soon after, Rosemary visited her college friend Karen Newsome in Charleston and urged Sergio to come for a visit. They fell in love with the city and quickly relocated, finding employment at Carolina's restaurant. They purchased the 1794 brick carriage house at 79½ Anson Street as their residence.

1992. Rosemary and Sergio entered negotiations to purchase the Primrose Restaurant on East Bay Street from the Yaeger family. The sale nearly fell through due to antagonism between the Yaegers and Sergio. In fact, Joanne Yaeger thought that Sergio was dangerous, a "malignancy," but did not feel it was her place to tell Rosemary about her fears. However, Yaeger shared her fear of Sergio with others, including an official statement on record with her legal counsel. The attorney thought Yaeger was being paranoid, but he took her statement.

Rosemary was able to convince the Yaegers to sell, and the deal was concluded.

1994. Rosemary bought out another of the Yaegers' businesses and named it the Primrose Bakery. She and Sergio settled into a grueling work routine. Rosemary would leave the house by 4:00 a.m. to begin baking and finish around 2:00 p.m. She would stop by the restaurant to help. By 5:00 p.m., she was usually home and in bed by 8:00 p.m. Sergio's workday started around 10:00 a.m., and he rarely left the restaurant until midnight. That left them very little time for anything else but sleep.

SPRING OF 1994. Rosemary was invited to a National Culinary Arts Event in New York City with two other local, male chefs. Before her trip, Rosemary and Sergio took a week-long vacation to the Cayman Islands, which, according to Rosemary's friends, was a final attempt to rekindle their faltering marriage.

AUGUST 10, 1994. One week before her planned trip to New York, Rosemary left the restaurant around 5:00 p.m. At 5:15 p.m., Sergio left the restaurant to go to an Eckerd's Drugstore and returned half an hour later. Soon after that, Sergio burned himself with grease while cooking fish. He seemed agitated about the injury all night, pointing it out to everyone in the kitchen. He even called Rosemary at home to complain about it, but he noted to his friends that "she didn't answer the phone."

Sergio closed the restaurant early and went drinking at Vickery's with a friend, Peter Simmons. They arrived at 79½ Anson Street and noticed all the lights were on and the door was unlocked. Sergio was adamant that Simmons come inside because he insisted, "Something's wrong. She should be asleep."

Once inside, Sergio immediately went upstairs and yelled. Simmons ran upstairs and saw Rosemary's body on the floor. The carpet was soaked with blood; he ran downstairs and placed a 911 call. The two men waited in the driveway. Two officers arrived and Sergio told them, "My wife has been murdered—she's dead in the house."

One officer entered the house, and the second stayed outside. The second officer testified that Sergio made the comment, "Boy, what a bad day. I burned my face and now my wife has been murdered."

Within an hour, thirty officers were on the scene, including the medical examiner's office, the county coroner's office and city of Charleston police crime scene unit (CSU). Detectives found bloodstained bedding in the guest bedroom, as well as blood splatters on the carpet and walls. There was a pillow with powder burns and two gunshot holes. Overturned furniture was strewn about the room. A pair of bloody latex gloves lay on top of the chest of drawers.

Rosemary was clothed in a tee shirt, black underwear and red socks. Her ankles and wrists were bound behind her back. She had been shot at close range, once in the head and once in the back. She had been stabbed from behind thirty times. The attack was so brutal that almost her entire blood volume had drained from her body, soaked through the floor and walls and pooled onto the living room carpet downstairs.

Joann Yaeger had moved away from Charleston at this point, but she received a call from her former Charleston attorney. He apologized for thinking she had been an alarmist in her fear of Sergio. He told Yaeger he was convinced that Sergio was responsible for Rosemary's death.

Four days later, Sergio was arrested and charged with his wife's murder. Four months later, he walked out of Charleston County Jail free on bond with an electronic monitoring bracelet around his ankle.

Two weeks later, the TV program *Inside Edition* aired a segment about the murder, comparing the case with the June 1994 murder of O.J. Simpson's ex-wife Nicole Brown. Part of the story indicated there was some evidence that Sergio was a local cocaine dealer with powerful contacts in South America; another theory was that Sergio was also jealous of Rosemary's impending trip to New York with two other local male chefs.

The case against Sergio was presented to a grand jury three times, and each time Solicitor David P. Schwacke failed to get an indictment.

JANUARY 1995. Schwacke dropped the charges against Sergio, citing a lack of physical evidence, in particular "the presence of some unexplained DNA sample at the crime scene...some body fluid that is neither Sergio's nor Rosemary's."

As of today, the murder of Rosemary remains unsolved and open. The carriage house at 79½ Anson Street is currently a private home.

Chapter Nine

A Tragedy in Union
The Sad Saga of Susan Smith (1994)

This story needs little introduction, as it became a national media obsession, but most people know little of the details because they only know the surface sensational media coverage. This horrific crime is a far greater tragedy than it seemed on the surface. See the appendices for more documents that relate to this story.

OCTOBER 17, 1994. At age twenty-seven, Tom Findlay was considered to be the most eligible bachelor in Union, South Carolina. He was the son of the owner of Conso Products, the largest employer in town, and heir of the company. For most of 1994, he had been dating his father's assistant executive secretary, Susan Smith, but he had decided to break off the relationship.

Tom feared that the gulf between their backgrounds was too large to be crossed. He was the son of privilege, wealth and power, and she was the daughter of a millworker who had committed suicide when his wife divorced him. There was also a recent incident at a hot tub party that bothered him. Susan and the husband of one of her friends had climbed in the tub naked and proceeded to kiss and fondle each other. And then there was the matter of Susan's two small children from her current marriage. Tom was adamant that he did not want the responsibility of rearing someone else's children.

Tom wrote Susan a letter that was as much a cheerleading letter as it was a "Dear John." In the letter Tom told Susan, "You are intelligent, beautiful, sensitive, understanding, and possess many other wonderful qualities that I and many other men appreciate. You will, without a doubt, make some lucky man a great wife. But unfortunately, it won't be me."

He also wrote, "Susan, I could really fall for you. You have so many endearing qualities about you, and I think that you are a terrific person. But like I have told you before, there are some things about you that aren't suited for me, and yes, I am speaking about your children. I'm sure that your kids are good kids, but it really wouldn't matter how good they may be…the fact is, I just don't want children."

As far as Tom knew, the letter would be the end of their romantic relationship.

SEPTEMBER 26, 1971. Susan Leigh Vaughn was born in Union. Her father, Harry, was a fireman who later worked at a local textile mill. Her mother, Linda, was a homemaker. They married in 1960 when Ray was twenty years old. Linda was seventeen and pregnant with another man's child. That first son, Michael, was raised with Harry and Linda's two other children, Scotty and Susan.

Harry was an alcoholic with a violent temper. He was often convinced that Linda was being unfaithful, which pushed him into such rages that he threatened to kill Linda and himself. By the time Susan had started school, her older half-brother had attempted suicide by hanging. For years Michael would be treated for depression at Duke Medical Center and other facilities.

That was the household in which Susan grew up. In 1977, after years of violence and drunken arguments, Linda divorced Harry, which pushed him into heavier alcoholism. Two weeks after the divorce was final, Linda married Beverly (Bev) Russell, a wealthy businessman who had become a committeeman on the South Carolina State Republican Party and was on the advisory board of the Christian Coalition. Bev had several older daughters from his first marriage, and Susan, Scotty and Michael all moved into a new, larger house.

JANUARY 15, 1978. Five weeks after the divorce was final, Harry broke a window and entered Linda's house. Harry was so out of control that she called the police. Officers arrived to witness Harry striking Linda. Later that day, Harry committed suicide by placing a gun between his legs and pulling the trigger. It did not kill him immediately, but it was a mortal wound, and when he was brought to the hospital doctors could not save his life. For the rest of her life, two of Susan's most prized possessions would be Harry's coin collection and an audio recording of his voice. With the death of her father, Susan, always looking for male attention, began to focus on winning the approval of her stepfather, Bev. As Susan became a teenager, her mother often felt she was in competition with her daughter for Bev's affections.

When Susan was thirteen, she attempted suicide with an overdose of aspirin. In spite of the obvious dysfunction in the house and Susan's deep-seated troubled emotions, she did well in school. She was a member of the Beta Club, as well as the Math, Spanish and Red Cross Clubs. She was also president of the Junior Civitan Club at her high school.

In 1987, a few days before Susan's sixteenth birthday, one of Bev's older daughters had come to visit. Susan gave up her bedroom for the other woman and slept on the couch. When she was ready for bed, she discovered Bev sitting at one end of the sofa watching television. Susan crawled into Bev's lap and fell asleep. She was slowly awakened by the sensation of Bev's hand on her breasts. Bev took Susan's hand and placed it on his genitals. Susan was wide awake, but pretended to be asleep. She later told her mother she "wanted to see how far he would go."

A complaint was filed and investigated by the South Carolina Department of Social Services. Bev moved out of the house while the three of them— Bev, Linda and Susan—attended family counseling. However, after five sessions, they stopped going and Bev moved back in.

FEBRUARY 1988. Susan reported to her Union High School guidance counselor, Camille Stribling, that Bev Russell was molesting her. Stribling reported the allegations to social services, which investigated. Bev did not deny the allegations of French kissing, breast fondling and over-the-clothing masturbation. Bev's attorney reached an agreement with Assistant Circuit Solicitor Jack Flynn. The agreement was signed by Judge David Wilburn and sealed by the court, so the details of the agreement could never be made public.

During the summer between her junior and senior years, Susan began working at the local Winn-Dixie as a cashier. Within six months, she was head cashier and finally became the bookkeeper. By the end of the summer, she was having an affair with an older, married co-worker, and at the same time she was sleeping with *another* co-worker. She became pregnant and had an abortion. When the married man found about her affair with the second worker, he told her it was over between them.

NOVEMBER 1988. Susan again attempted suicide, this time with an extreme overdose of aspirin and Tylenol. She was hospitalized in Spartanburg Regional Medical Center for a week. She was allowed to return to Winn-Dixie after she recovered, where she became friendly with one of the stock clerks, David Smith. Susan and David had known each other at Union High, but they grew friendly over the next two years.

During her senior year at Union High School, Susan was voted "Friendliest Female." She wore miniskirts and tight blouses; she was outgoing and vivacious. After graduation, she and David began to date, even though he was already involved with another woman.

JANUARY 1991. Susan told David that she was pregnant. David told his fiancé Christy about Susan, and she immediately broke off the engagement. David and Susan decided to marry, since neither of them wanted an abortion. Even though Susan wanted to marry, that meant she would have to give up college. She wanted to go, but did not know what she wanted to study, so she decided to marry David instead.

Susan's mother and Bev were not happy about the pregnancy and marriage. Susan was nineteen and David was twenty. The wedding was set for March 15, 1991, despite their disapproval.

David had grown up in a strained household. His mother, Barbara, was a strict Jehovah's Witness. David's father, Charles Smith, grew to intensely dislike his wife's fervent religious views. At age seventeen, David escaped the strained atmosphere of his parents' house and moved next door with his great-grandmother. There was a small house on the property that had been empty for years. David began to work on the house, and over the next few years he slowly transformed it into habitable condition. When he and Susan became engaged, David showed Susan the house and told her of his plans to move in after the wedding. Susan agreed, until Bev and Linda came over to see the house. After that visit, Susan claimed it was nothing more than a "tin-roofed country shack." Susan agreed to live with David in his great-grandmother's house instead of the house he had constructed.

Eleven days before the wedding, David's older brother, Danny, died of complications of Crohn's disease. Even though David's family was dealing with the grief, Linda insisted that the wedding take place as scheduled. If they waited much longer, Susan's pregnancy would begin to show.

After the wedding, David and Susan felt the pressure of married life, particularly in a financial sense. Together, they had an income of $40,000, but Susan enjoyed material things so much that she often borrowed money from her mother to pay their bills. That angered David, as he and Linda did not get along. David felt Linda was too controlling. She often dropped by the house unannounced and preached to them how to live and get along and deal with their problems.

MAY 1991. David's father, Charles, attempted suicide by an overdose of pills. Susan came home from work and found him. He was hospitalized and treated for depression. His wife, Barbara, moved to Myrtle Beach.

OCTOBER 10, 1991. Michael Daniel Smith was born. The middle name was chosen in honor of David's older brother. But even the birth did not smooth over the rocky relationship between Susan and David. They both worked in the same Winn-Dixie, and David was her boss. A few days after their first anniversary, they separated. Susan began a relationship with her former Winn-Dixie lover, until she and David reconciled and moved back in together. However, within a few months they were separated again. They went back and forth for almost a year.

NOVEMBER 1992. Susan became pregnant with David's second child. They decided to give the relationship one more chance. Bev and Linda gave them the money for a down payment on a ranch-style house at 407 Toney Road in Union. As the pregnancy progressed, Susan became moody and complained about being "fat and ugly." She shut David out completely, and by June 1993 he had begun an affair with one of his cashiers.

AUGUST 5, 1993. Alexander Tyler Smith was born by emergency cesarean. Three months later, David moved out of the house and back in with his great-grandmother. They had decided the marriage was over.

After she recovered from her surgery, Susan went to find a new job. She refused to go back to Winn-Dixie, where David would be her boss and she would have to work with his new girlfriend. She found a job as assistant to the executive secretary for J. Carey Findlay, president and CEO of Conso Products. Founded in 1867, Conso was originally a millinery trimmings company, but when Susan got her job it was the largest manufacturer in the world of decorative trimmings for the home furnishings industry.

Susan's job gave her the responsibility of arranging travel details for company employees as well as for clients from all over the world. It introduced her to an entire new group of friends—a more professional, upscale group. She became part of a regular clique that congregated at Hickory Nuts, a nightclub in Union. She also met the boss's son, Tom Findlay. He had graduated from Auburn University and taken a job as head of the graphic arts department at Conso. He lived in a cottage on his father's estate.

Starting in January 1994, Susan and Tom began to date, meeting for lunch or going to the movies. Susan also attended several parties at Tom's cottage. However, she was feeling a strain. She was working a new job, had custody of her two sons, was going through a divorce and taking a part-time course load at the University of South Carolina. She was also juggling a sexual relationship with three men—Tom; her ex-husband, David; and her stepfather, Bev Russell. She was drinking heavily and missing work. She often felt depressed and anxious.

She began to constantly wear one of Tom's Auburn University sweatshirts, and by the end of the summer Susan was more hopeful. She believed that her dreams of happiness and stability might finally be answered with

Tom. Tom, however, was beginning to have other ideas. He felt Susan was becoming possessive and needy. He decided to compose a letter for her. He was feeling suffocated, pressured and wished to end the relationship as gently, but as firmly, as possible.

OCTOBER 21, 1994. Three days after she received Tom's "Dear Susan" letter, divorce papers for Susan and David Smith were filed at the Union County Courthouse.

OCTOBER 23, 1994. Two days after reading the letter, Susan arrived at Tom's cottage. She was angry, hurt, bitter and most of all confused. She poured out the details of her relationship with Bev Russell, how it had started and continued through all those years. Instead being sympathetic, as she hoped, Tom was shocked and disgusted by the sordid tale. It only confirmed his decision to end his relationship with her.

OCTOBER 25, 1994. Susan dressed Michael and Alex and took them to day care. She went to work and had lunch with a group of Conso employees, including Tom Findlay.

After lunch, Susan asked Sandy Williams, her supervisor, if she could go home early.

"What's wrong?" Sandy asked.

"I'm in love with someone who doesn't love me," Susan said sadly.

"Who?"

"Tom Findlay," Susan said, "but it can never be because of my children."

Instead of going home, Susan decided to stay at work. She called Tom and asked him to meet her outside the building to talk. Reluctantly, he agreed.

Susan told him, "David is threatening to make public some embarrassing things about me during our divorce."

"Like what?"

"Like I have been cheating the IRS," she said, and then dropped a bombshell of a lie. "And having an affair with your father."

Tom was shocked into silence for a moment and then told her, "We can stay friends, but our intimate affair will have to stop forever."

Before 5:00 p.m., Susan went to find Tom and tried to return the Auburn sweatshirt. He told her to keep it.

Susan picked up Michael and Alex from day care and then drove by the after work hangout, Hickory Nuts. A co-worker, Sue Brown, had just pulled her car into the parking lot. Susan asked Sue to do a favor for her. She needed to return to Conso to speak with Tom, and wanted Sue to watch her children while she went in the building.

"I have to apologize to Tom," Susan said. "I just wanted to see his reaction, so I told him that I was having an affair with his father. I have to apologize."

The women drove back to Conso in Susan's car. Susan went inside, and when Tom saw her he frowned and led her outside. A few minutes later, Susan came out and got in the car. As she drove Sue Brown back to Hickory Nuts, she was visibly upset. When Sue got out of the car, Susan said, "I may just end it," and drove away.

At 8:00 p.m., Susan dressed Michael and Alex, put them in the backseat of her Mazda and began to drive around Union. She later said that she had "never felt so lonely and sad in my life." She drove down Highway 49 to John D. Long Lake. She drove halfway down the seventy-five-foot boat ramp and parked in the middle. The headlights were on and both boys were in the back seat, sleeping, strapped in their car seats.

Susan shifted the car into neutral and felt it begin to roll down the remaining forty feet. She put her foot on the brake and stopped the car. She pulled up the emergency brake, got out of the car and released the emergency brake. She watched the car slowly roll into the John D. Long Lake. For the next few minutes, she stood on the boat ramp and watched the car bob on the surface. It finally began to sink into the dark water. Susan watched until all that was visible were the dimming lights. Then she turned and ran toward a nearby house.

About 9:00 p.m., Shirley McCloud was reading the local newspaper when she heard a sound on her front porch, a sobbing, wailing sound of anguish. Shirley switched on the front porch light, which illuminated a hysterical young woman, sobbing. The young woman screamed, "Please help me! He's got my kids and he's got my car!"

Shirley put her arm around the woman and walked her into the house. The young woman sobbed, "A black man has got my kids and my car."

They called 911.

Once Susan had calmed down, she told Shirley the following story. She had been driving her 1990 Mazda through town, and while she was stopped at the red light by Monarch Mills a black man jumped in the car, pointed a gun at her and told her to drive. Susan asked, "Why are you doing this?" and he replied, "Shut up and drive, or I'll kill you."

She drove four miles northeast out of Union until he made her "stop right past the sign."

"The John D. Long Lake sign?" Shirley asked. The sign was only several hundred yards away from Shirley's house.

Susan answered, "Yes."

The black man told her to get out. "Why can't I take my kids?" Susan asked. He replied, "I don't have time."

Susan said he pointed the gun at her and then pushed her out of the car. "Don't worry," he told Susan, "I'm not going to hurt your kids." He drove away with her two young sons in the back seat.

A few minutes later—Susan was not sure how long she lay on the ground crying—she got up and began to run until she got to Shirley McCloud's porch. Susan asked to use the bathroom and to call her mother. Her mother didn't answer the phone, so she called her stepfather and then her soon-to-be ex-husband.

By the time Susan was talking to David, the Union County Sheriff, Howard Wells, had arrived and begun to organize the search for the children. Sheriff Wells knew Susan Smith; he and his wife Wanda were good friends with Susan's brother, Scotty Vaughn, and his wife, Wendy.

The sheriff asked Susan to repeat the story, even though he had already heard it from the 911 dispatcher and from Shirley McCloud. Wells took notes as Susan talked. He noted her face was red and puffy; she sat with her hands clasped in her lap. She was wearing a gray Auburn University sweatshirt. Wells asked for descriptions of the children. Michael, age three, was wearing a white jogging suit, and Alex, age fourteen months, was dressed in a red- and white-striped outfit.

Wells quickly realized that the resources of the Union County law enforcement were not going to be enough in the search for the boys and the Mazda. He called SLED to assist as quickly as possible. Within twenty-four hours there were over one thousand people actively involved in the search for Michael and Alex Smith.

When Susan's family began to descend on the McClouds' house, Sheriff Wells suggested the family find another place to gather, so they all moved to Susan's mother's house. Susan rode with David from the McClouds' house. She told him, "Tom Findlay might come to see me. I don't want you to get upset if he does."

David was puzzled that his soon-to-be ex-wife was more concerned about David's reaction to Tom's impending visit than the kidnapping of her sons, but he wrote it off as an odd sign of her stress.

OCTOBER 26, 1994. The search for the boys continued, and the Adam Walsh Center in Columbia, South Carolina, got involved. The Center was named for six-year-old Adam Walsh, who disappeared from a Florida Sears store while shopping with his mother.

The Columbia Center's director wanted to speak to Susan and David and drove to Union. While this was happening, a SLED helicopter with heat sensors flew over John D. Long Lake and divers searched part of the lake. Sheriff Wells needed a better description of the kidnapper, so he brought in a police sketch artist. The black man Susan described was about forty years old and wore a dark knit cap, jeans and a plaid shirt.

Linda's house was soon filled with relatives and friends. Tom Findlay called to talk to Susan. As they discussed the missing children, Susan began to talk about *their* relationship. Tom encouraged her to forget about them, she should just concentrate on her children. Later, when a group of Conso employees came to visit, Susan pulled Sue Brown off to the side. "When is Tom coming to visit, do you know?" she asked. Sue said she had no idea.

The story of the abduction had at first only been covered by the local newspaper and radio, but the story began to branch out. National morning shows like *Today* and *Good Morning, America* mentioned the story. Margaret Frierson and Charlotte Foster of the Adam Walsh Center arrived and met with Susan, David, Bev, Linda and Scotty. They offered to be the liaison between the family and the media, to schedule interviews and supply pictures of the boys for broadcast news.

David, Susan and Margaret then went to the sheriff's office for another interview with police. Wells and SLED officer Eddie Harris suggested that the parents make a plea for the safe return of the boys via the national media.

That evening, David stood on the steps of the Union Sheriff's Department with Susan by his side and made a statement.

> *To whoever has our boys, we ask that you please don't hurt them and bring them back. We love them very much…I plead to the guy please return our children to us safe and unharmed. Everywhere I look I see their play toys and pictures. They are both wonderful children. I don't know how else to put it. And I can't imagine life without them.*

After the statement, Susan was questioned for six more hours by SLED agents. She was asked to repeat the details of her story over and over. Sheriff Wells asked David Caldwell to drive from Columbia to interview Susan. Caldwell was the director of the Forensic Sciences Laboratory for SLED.

OCTOBER 27, 1994. David and Susan were given polygraph tests and signed a form that advised them of their Miranda rights. David's test showed he knew nothing about the kidnapping. Susan's test was inconclusive. When she was asked, "Do you know where your children are?" her response showed a high level of deception. This was the first of many polygraph tests Susan was given.

During the day, Agent Caldwell interviewed Susan three times. She was given a polygraph each time. Caldwell was concerned about several inconsistencies in her story. Susan had claimed she was sitting at a red light in the Monarch Mills intersection. However, that light remained green unless a car on the crossing street triggered the change to red. The light would have been green unless there was another car at the intersection, and thus, police surmised, there would have been a witness to the carjacking.

Susan also claimed to be in Wal-Mart that evening with the boys, but no one in the store remembered seeing them there. And another odd thing bothered the investigators: where was Susan's car? By this time it should have been found—either abandoned or pulled over by a policeman—unless it had been purposely hidden. They also discovered that David and Susan had filed for divorce, and that Susan was dating several other men. Agents interviewed Tom Findlay, who gave them a copy of the "Dear Susan" letter.

Caldwell later confronted Susan with the knowledge that Tom had broken off their relationship because of her children. "Did this fact play any role or have any bearing on the disappearance of your children?"

Susan answered, "No man would make me hurt my children. They were my life!" To investigators, the fact that Susan referred to her children in the past tense—"They *were* my life"—indicated that she thought her sons were dead.

When Caldwell repeated her statement about her children's fussiness, he asked, "Is *that* why you killed them?"

Susan slammed her fist on the table. "You son of a bitch! How can you think that? I can't believe you think I did it!"

Caldwell also noted that Susan often cried, but no tears were ever present during her sobbing. "Fake sounds of crying with no tears in her eyes," one agent noted in his report. Caldwell also asked the FBI to work up a profile of a homicidal mother. The profile fit Susan so accurately it was uncanny: "A woman in her twenties, who grew up and/or lived in poverty, under-educated with a history of physical and/or sexual abuse. Has depressive and suicidal tendencies, and has suffered recent male rejection at the time of the murder."

That day, Sheriff Wells was a guest on the *Today* show on NBC and *Larry King Live* on CNN. He reported that divers had searched John D. Long Lake and found nothing. However, divers were working under a false assumption. Everyone was thinking the car would have been driven into the lake at a high speed. The faster a car hits the water, the more waves it creates, which stops forward momentum. That car would sink close to the bank. No one considered the possibility that a car driven slowly into the water would float and drift farther out. So while divers were only searching the water close to the shore, the Mazda was sitting at the bottom of the lake one hundred feet away.

OCTOBER 28, 1994. Sheriff Wells announced to the public that there were no solid clues and no suspect had been ruled out, including the parents, David and Susan Smith.

OCTOBER 29, 1994. One aspect of the story that bothered many people in Union was the racial angle. Given the intense media and law enforcement scrutiny of the case, how could a black man in a stolen car with two white children remain at large for so long?

By this time, the investigators had concluded that Susan was lying about her involvement. Most thought it was a custody issue, and Susan had merely hidden them from David, but others were thinking the worst—she had killed her children. How and why they did not know, but the next issue was how they could get her to confess.

Susan was being interviewed several times a day. The investigators' plan was to slowly break her down to the point where she was so tired and confused that she could be coaxed into revealing the truth. She was given a polygraph at each interview and always failed the question, "Do you know where your children are?" Meanwhile, thousands of officials and volunteers still searched for the boys.

NOVEMBER 1, 1994. One week had passed since the boys were kidnapped. Sheriff Wells met with reporters. "I don't know that we're any closer to finding the car," he said.

SLED officials encouraged *America's Most Wanted*, hosted by John Walsh, to film a segment about the kidnapping, hoping the increasing media pressure would push Susan into confessing. A group of ministers were encouraged to give a press conference to make an appeal to the carjacker.

NOVEMBER 3, 1994. David and Susan appeared on all three major network television morning shows. Even though they were legally separated, they sat side by side in Bev and Linda's living room holding hands, the model picture of a young grieving couple in love. When Susan was asked if she had any involvement in her children's disappearance, she said, "I did not have anything to do with the abduction of my children. Whoever did this is a *sick and emotionally unstable person.*" (author's emphasis)

David was asked if he believed his wife. "Yes, I believe my wife totally."

SLED agent Eddie Harris was assigned to drive Susan from the house to her sessions with officers for questioning. After her appearance on television,

Harris drove Susan to meet with Sheriff Wells. The agent was stunned when Susan asked him, "How did I look on TV?"

At 1:40 p.m., Susan met Wells in a room at the First Baptist Church in Union. He told her flat out, "I know your story about the black carjacker is a lie." He told Susan that he was going to announce to the media that the carjacker story was false because it was creating tension in the black community.

Susan looked at the sheriff for a moment. "Will you pray with me?" she asked.

They prayed for a moment, and Wells ended it by saying, "Lord, we know that all things will be revealed in time." He then opened his eyes, looked at Susan and told her, "Susan, it is time."

Susan began to cry. "I am so ashamed, I am so ashamed. Can I have your gun so I can kill myself?"

"Why would you want to do that?"

"You don't understand. My children are not all right."

Over the next sixty minutes, Susan poured out the entire story of recent events in her life. She wrote out a two-page confession of how she killed her two sons. She claimed her original intention had been to commit suicide; all three of them were going to die together. She felt her children would "be better off with me and God than if they were left without a mother and alone."

But she hadn't committed suicide. She had gotten out of the car, released the brake and sent her sons to the bottom of the lake. She told Wells where to find the car.

Divers were sent immediately back out to John D. Long Lake. Using the new information about where to look, Curtis Jackson and Mike Gault paddled a small boat out into the lake. Jackson dove once but came up with no success. He dove again, and six minutes into his second dive he located the underside of a car. His light was not powerful enough to cut through the dark gloom of eighteen feet of water, so he surfaced. The fact that Susan was so accurate on the location of the car chilled the divers involved. That meant she had stood and watched the car sink. She had watched her children die.

A second team of divers arrived. Steve Morrow and Francis Mitchum possessed more sophisticated underwater lights, so they went down to the car. Morrow later told Sheriff Wells that the children "were in car seats hanging upside down. I was able to determine one occupant on either side of the car."

Sheriff Wells immediately returned to Bev and Linda's home in Union. For the next twenty minutes, Wells told the family the harrowing truth.

Susan had driven her car into the lake with Michael and Alex strapped to their car seats. Susan was arrested and charged with two counts of murder. She would be arraigned the next day at the Union County Court House.

At 5:00 p.m., Wells held the now famous national news conference in which he announced that Susan Smith had murdered her two sons. It sent shock waves across the nation. He then returned to John D. Long Lake to be present when the car was recovered. The windshield had cracked from the water pressure and temperature changes at the bottom of the lake. The bodies of Michael and Alex Smith were placed in an ambulance and taken to the Medical University of South Carolina Medical Center in Charleston.

NOVEMBER 4, 1994. The autopsies of the boys revealed that both had been alive when the car entered the lake. They had both drowned. That evening, at a Union town meeting, more than one hundred blacks and whites met as a symbol of unity, good will and comfort. Susan's brother, Scotty, officially apologized to the black community on behalf of the family.

Susan was moved to the Women's Correctional Facility in Columbia and placed on a twenty-four-hour suicide watch. That night in her six- by fourteen-foot cell, Susan wrote David a letter that was filled with the phrase, "I'm sorry."

NOVEMBER 6, 1994. The funeral for Michael and Alex Smith was held at Buffalo United Methodist Church. The brothers were buried together in a white casket next to the uncle that neither boy had ever met—David's older brother, Danny.

Susan was held without bond at the York County Jail. Bev and Linda hired David Brock as Susan's attorney. Brock was a South Carolina lawyer who specialized in death penalty cases. Eventually, Bev and Linda had to mortgage their home to pay for Brock's services.

JANUARY 16, 1995. Union County Solicitor Thomas Pope filed a notice of intention to seek the death penalty against Susan Smith.

FEBRUARY 1995. Bev and Linda separated. Bev Russell resigned from his position at the South Carolina Republican executive committee.

MAY 1995. David and Susan's divorce became final. Susan waived her right to attend. David and Susan divided the children's toys and clothes. David also received the Mazda. After Susan's trial, he had the car destroyed.

JUNE 18, 1995. Father's Day. Bev wrote a letter to Susan. "My heart breaks for what I have done to you. I want you to know that you do not have all the guilt for this tragedy."

JULY 7, 1995. Susan's minister, Mark Long, announced that Susan had been baptized and undergone a Christian conversion. Very few people believed it.

JULY 10, 1995. Susan Smith was put on trial for the murder of her two sons. David Brock advised Susan to plead guilty to both charges and be sentenced to thirty years without parole. Solicitor Pope rejected the plea bargain.

JULY 22, 1995. Closing arguments. Solicitor Pope told the jury that Susan Smith had "used the emergency brake handle like a gun, and eliminated her toddlers so that she could have a chance at a life with Tom Findlay, the man she said she loved."

The defense stated that "this is not a case about evil, but a case of sadness and despair. Susan had choices in her life, but her choices were irrational and her choices were tragic."

After a two-and-a-half-hour deliberation, the jury returned with a verdict of guilty on two counts of murder.

JULY 27, 1995. Penalty Phase. The same jury that found Susan guilty rejected the death sentence and recommended that she spend the rest of her life in prison. Judge Howard sentenced Susan Smith to thirty years in prison. She will be eligible for parole in 2025, when she will be fifty-three years old.

David Smith publicly stated that he disagreed with the sentence. He said, "Justice was not served because Susan was not sentenced to death."

Even after she was sent to prison, the drama did not end in Susan Smith's life.

Second Guard Arrested for Sex with Susan Smith
Inmate Informed Prison Authorities of Liaison
Sept. 26, 2000
COLUMBIA, S.C. (AP)—A second prison guard has been arrested for allegedly having sex with Susan Smith, who is serving a life sentence for drowning her two sons in a lake. Capt. Alfred R. Rowe Jr. was charged Monday with one count of sexual intercourse with an inmate, punishable by up to 10 years in prison. His arraignment was scheduled for today.

Smith told investigators she had sex with Rowe at the Women's Correctional Institution between July and August. He confessed, according to an arrest warrant.

Mug shot of Susan Smith. *Courtesy of the South Carolina Department of Corrections.*

A woman who answered at a Columbia telephone number given for Rowe said he did not live there. Prosecutors said Rowe was a supervisor who worked with the Corrections Department about 13 years. Charges that another guard, Lt. Houston Cagle, had sex with Smith triggered the investigation that revealed the second encounter.

The first encounter was discovered when Smith was treated for a sexually transmitted disease, prosecutors have said. Corrections Department spokesman John Barkley refused to comment on whether she had a sexually transmitted disease but said Smith was not pregnant. Smith was sentenced to life in prison after drowning her two sons in a South Carolina lake in 1994. She had staged the boys' disappearance as a kidnapping and pleaded tearfully for their safe return on national television broadcasts.

The emotional impact that the Susan Smith tragedy had on America is illustrated by the number of cultural references it has inspired.

Musician Hayden's song "When This Is Over" (from the 1995 album *Everything I Long For*) views the murders from the point of view of three-year-old Michael Smith.

Blind Melon's song "Car Seat (God's Presents)" from their 1995 album *Soup* is about the murder.

The 1995 episode of *Law & Order* entitled "Angel" was based on the Susan Smith case. In the episode, a young mother blames a Puerto Rican man for the disappearance of her baby. The Smith case is referred to specifically in both the investigation and the eventual trial.

There is an episode of *South Park* in which Butters's mother tries to murder him. She later blames "some Puerto Rican guy."

Poet Lee Ann Brown's "The Ballad of Susan Smith" is a sung poem set to an old Southern mountain hymn tune.

The Susan Smith case is referred to in the third season opener of *Arrested Development*. In the episode, Lucille Bluth, freshly off her antidepressants in a flashback, cheers up when hearing the news of Susan Smith's murder of her children. At the end of the episode, Lucille accidentally lets her car roll into a lake with her son Buster sleeping inside.

Richard Price's novel *Freedomland* and the subsequent 2006 film starring Samuel L. Jackson and Julianne Moore is loosely based on the Susan Smith case. The plot: late one night in a working-class New Jersey suburb, a bloodied woman staggers dazed into the emergency room at the Dempsy Medical Center and claims she was forced out of her car by a black man. After further questioning by police, she finally breaks down and reveals that her four-year-old son, Cody, was asleep in the back seat of the stolen car.

And if that is not enough, there is this story from September 1996. It looks as though the tragedy in Union will haunt that city, and others, for a long time to come.

Union, SC Lake Takes Seven More Lives
By Gary Karr
UNION, S.C. (AP)—A family and friends visiting the spot where Susan Smith drowned her two little boys met with tragedy themselves when their vehicle rolled into John D. Long Lake. Three adults and four children drowned.

Five of the victims were from one family—parents and their three children.

"It's like it's haunted or something. It keeps taking lives," Tommy Vinson, 46, said Sunday as he stood beside the lake a half-dozen miles outside town.

The accident happened late Saturday. State divers worked through the night to find the bodies in the water near the boat ramp where Ms. Smith killed her children.

The group of 10 had driven out to the lake and parked next to the ramp with their Chevrolet Suburban's headlights shining on two memorials to the Smith boys, 3-year-old Michael and 14-month-old Alex, Sheriff Howard Wells told WSPA-TV.

Five of the group had gotten out of the vehicle when it started to roll toward the water with four children and an adult inside, said Mike Willis, a spokesman for the state Natural Resources Department.

It passed between the memorial markers and knocked over a young tree planted in the Smith boys' memory as it slid down the steep grassy embankment into about 15 feet of water.

Two adults—parents of three of the children—dived into the lake to help, and drowned with the others.

"There's going to be some who say the lake needs to be drained. There should have been guardrails built," said Leonard Roark, a retired textile worker from Union who was among those gathered at the lake Sunday morning.

The accident killed an entire family from nearby Buffalo: Tim Phillips, 28; his wife, Angie, 22; and Courtney, 4; Melena, 23 months, and 4-month-old Kinsleigh, said Teresa Mims, the Phillips' cousin.

Tim and Angie Phillips were the ones who jumped into the water trying to save their children and the others, said Bobby Moore, a neighbor of Phillips' mother, Patsy Phillips.

Neither he nor Ms. Mims knew the identity of the other two victims. The Union County Sheriff's Department would not release their identities.

On Oct. 25, 1994, Ms. Smith, distraught over a love affair, released the safety brake on her car and let it roll down the boat ramp with her sons still strapped inside in the back seat.

For nine days, she insisted that a black man had commandeered her car, and she begged tearfully on nationwide television for her sons' safe return. On Nov. 3, she confessed that she had drowned the boys.

Ms. Smith was sentenced in July 1995 to life in prison. She will be eligible for parole in 2025.

Union, a town of 10,000 people, is roughly 55 miles northwest of Columbia.

In May of 1999, Mary Ferguson Cunningham drove her car into the lake committing suicide. It was the 10th death in the lake in less than 5 years.

Chapter Ten

Obsession
The Death of Mary Lynn Witherspoon (2003)

This story is of a neighborhood that has almost no violent crime—South of Broad in Charleston. In this case, after Mary Lynn's murder, the victim's family was inspired to change the system. This story was featured on NBC's Dateline *on November 8, 2006.*

I f somebody asked you to list all the good qualities you could think of— brains, beauty, fairness. I would bet they would all apply to Mary Lynn Witherspoon," her friend Stanley Feldman said.

It did seem as if Mary Lynn had lived a charmed life. She was a beauty queen, made straight As on report cards and graduated as the high school valedictorian. After college, she became a popular French teacher at an exclusive private school, and married a doctor.

She lived in the most exclusive area of Charleston, South Carolina, called South of Broad, a neighborhood that boasts hundreds of homes built during Charleston's so-called "golden age" of a more mannered time. Charleston is often called a jewel of a Southern city, and if that is true, then South of Broad shines the brightest. It boasts hundreds of architecturally stunning homes built during the 1800s. The streets are narrow and clean; every yard is well groomed and protected by charming (yet imposing) wrought-iron gates and fences. The houses boast large verandas and piazzas for socializing, and the windows are shuttered as protection against the many coastal storms and prying eyes. South of Broad inspires the same protocol as a museum—you can look, but do not touch. That tranquility is often accented by the clip-clop of animal-drawn carriages carrying hundreds of thousands of tourists annually to gawk at this glimpse of an unreal world.

This was Mary Lynn Witherspoon's world; she had been a longtime presence in Charleston society. She could have easily spent her days in a leisurely manner, shopping, lunching and hosting bridge parties, but she loved children and enjoyed teaching, particularly sharing her passion for French with students.

When Mary Lynn Witherspoon divorced, she blossomed in the role of a single mother and embraced all that was good about Charleston. She particularly loved her French Huguenot Church, the only such congregation in the United States. Her daughter Jane said, "She taught me the right things to do…she had me in Sunday school and church and wanted me to surround myself with good people. And she modeled all of those behaviors herself."

As a single woman, Mary Lynn had no lack of suitors. She had to "beat them off with a stick. I think they all wanted to marry her," Feldman said.

1981. Edmonds Brown III was the most persistent suitor. He was the father of two children, Edmonds Tennent Brown IV—whom they called Tennent—age ten, and Molly, who was eight.

Jane said, "Edmonds was a wonderful man to me. He would come over in the morning and my mom would scoot out of the door. And he would come in and fix my breakfast and take me to school."

Brown and Mary Lynn seemed to be a good fit. Brown proposed over and over, and Mary Lynn said "no" each time—not because she did not care for him, but because she felt a strong uneasiness about joining the families.

Jackie Olsen, Mary Lynn's sister said, "Something was off. I think, deep in her heart, she realized it was not a situation that was going to be the best for her and Jane…Edmonds's daughter was so jealous of Jane and they just did not get along."

One of the things that "was off" was Brown's ten-year-old son. Tennent was often described by teachers as a "sweet child" who was always sad. He was lured to people who teased and picked on him, as if he was inviting punishment and ridicule.

Olsen said, "He wanted to be sweet. He wanted to be kind. He wanted people to love him." Jane called Tennent a "social misfit, even from a very young age."

Brown tried to get his son psychological help, but therapists never could diagnose anything that was wrong with him, except he was always sad. But Tennent loved Mary Lynn, and she tried to befriend the boy, but sensed something in him that led to her vague wariness.

1988. After seven years of dating and several rejected marriage proposals, Edmonds Brown and Mary Lynn broke off their relationship. But Tennent, by then in his late teens, still hovered. He was often seen standing on the sidewalk, staring at Mary Lynn's house. He rode his bicycle past the house and stood on the porch. Mary Lynn would speak to him cordially, but she never encouraged him. She never invited the boy into the house. He was never threatening, but he was always there.

1989. Mary Lynn moved to Mount Pleasant, a community east of the Cooper River from downtown Charleston.

"Tennent just popped up there at that house," Jane said. "And I have no idea how he knew that we had moved, and where we lived."

Mary Lynn went to visit her mother, who lived in another city. On the day she was to return to Charleston, Mary Lynn and her mother went for a walk. When they returned to her mother's house, they realized that someone had broken into the house during their absence, but nothing seemed to have been taken. Mary Lynn grabbed her suitcase and headed back to Charleston. When she unpacked her bag, she discovered her clothes and makeup had been stolen.

Mary Lynn's mother knew immediately who the thief was. She called Tennent Brown and told him, "I know that you broke in and that you got Mary Lynn's things out of her suitcase. Now bring them back."

He did. He placed them in a bag and left it on Mary Lynn's carport.

1991. Suddenly, Tennent was gone from Mary Lynn's life. He had joined the coast guard, and for the next eight years, Tennent Brown completely faded from Mary Lynn's thoughts. She moved back downtown to a small home on Tradd Street on the Charleston peninsula. She continued to teach French and to take some of her students to Europe during the summer. She remained active in the French Huguenot Church. Jane married and moved to Florida.

2001. Tennent returned. One afternoon, Mary Lynn saw him standing on the sidewalk across from her home. After a moment, he turned and left. Mary Lynn felt that fear again, but this time it was not so vague. Tennent Brown was no longer an odd, sad child; he was now an odd thirty-year-old man.

Over the next months, Tennent resumed his appearances on Tradd Street to stare at Mary Lynn's house. Friends called Edmonds Brown and urged him to "do something about this kid. He's driving Mary Lynn crazy. He's stalking her."

But Brown had had little contact with his son for years. So he did nothing.

Friends and family urged Mary Lynn to call police, but she responded that he had not committed a crime. However, she did discuss the situation with several local policemen, and they agreed to keep an eye on her house.

Mary Lynn Witherspoon's home on Tradd Street. *Photo by author.*

2002. Tennent was arrested for an auto theft charge, and part of his sentence included mental evaluation. Doctors diagnosed him as bipolar and suffering from a rare brain disorder called Asperger's syndrome, which prevented him from understanding the social significance of his words and behavior. Odder still, psychiatrists decided he suffered from gender dysphoria, a confusion of what gender he really was. Tennent was put on medication for his bipolar disorder.

APRIL 2003. Mary Lynn went to get clothes out of her dryer in the outside utility room, and all of her underwear was missing from the dryer. Of course, Mary Lynn knew who had taken her garments, but she chose not to call police. Instead, she installed an expensive and sophisticated alarm system. She also purchased pepper spray to carry with her.

JULY 2003. Mary Lynn came home one afternoon and Tennent was standing in the backyard. She spoke to him. "I'm sorry I can't visit, I'm running to PTA." She went inside, changed clothes and left.

The next afternoon when she came home and looked out the window, he was there again, except this time he was carrying a pillowcase full of her clothes. After a few minutes of staring at each other, Tennent walked out of the yard.

Shaking with fear, Mary Lynn called her sister, Jackie. "She was fearful. You could hear it in her voice," Jackie said. Then Jackie told her older sister, "He knows you know that it was him and if you don't do something, what is he gonna do if he comes back?"

Mary Lynn called the police. They picked Tennent up and charged him with burglary. When they ran a background check, they discovered he had a list of prior crimes: car theft and breaking and entering. Due to that record, he was not given bail, so he sat in jail waiting for trial. Authorities took several months trying to decide what to do with Tennent—put him in prison or give mental health treatment. No matter which, at some point Tennent would be back out on the streets, so Mary Lynn signed up for the Victim Notification System, VINE. She would be notified if Tennent were transferred to another facility, or if he was released. Someone would call her immediately, and a letter would be mailed to her.

NOVEMBER 4, 2003. Tennent pleaded guilty to the burglary charge of Mary Lynn's house. He was ordered by the judge to seek mental health treatment.

NOVEMBER 10, 2003. Tennent was released from jail and sent to an outpatient mental health clinic. He walked out of jail carrying a sheaf of papers one inch thick and went to visit a mental health counselor. Before he left, the counselor asked for Tennent's address, and he gave Mary Lynn's Tradd Street number as his address. The counselor told him to return on Wednesday for a counseling session.

Tennent walked out a free man.

NOVEMBER 14, 2003. Jane, in Florida, got a phone call from one of Mary Lynn's friends. She told Jane that Mary Lynn had not shown up for work that morning at school, and she had not arranged for a substitute. Jane knew immediately that something was wrong.

The school principal and another staff member went to the Tradd Street house. Mary Lynn's car was gone. They knocked on the door. No answer. Jane and her husband were in their car driving to Charleston. Over the phone, Jane authorized the police to enter the house. When they opened the door, they knew something had gone wrong.

Sergeant Barry Goldstein of the Charleston Police Department said, "Mary Lynn was a person that kept a very well-kept house. And in the kitchen there was still some food on a plate. Eggs on a plate in the kitchen. We discovered shoes. An apple. Her watch lying on the floor."

Police moved through the house and up the stairs. One of the balusters was kicked loose. They walked into the second-floor dressing room and into chaos. "There was a lot of personal property," Goldstein said. Drawers and closets had been rifled through; items were tossed all over the room.

They found Mary Lynn's body in the tub in the second-floor bathroom. She was naked. Her hands and feet were bound behind her with tape. She was dead—strangled, it looked. She had also been raped. A knife was lying nearby.

Police tape was draped around the house; the street was blocked with emergency vehicles flashing lights. Detectives were canvassing the neighborhood. This was not a common event South of Broad. In North Charleston, yes, where the violent crime rate is number ten in the United States, but not in *this* neighborhood. The difference between North Charleston and South of Broad is like South Central Los Angeles and Martha's Vineyard.

Police reconstructed the crime scene. They decided the assailant had confronted Mary Lynn as she was leaving for school in the morning. They struggled in the kitchen, and he forcibly carried or dragged her up the stairs, breaking one of the balusters. Once upstairs he tied her, raped her and strangled her. He then placed the body in the tub, went downstairs and cooked several eggs for his breakfast.

Everyone in the family suspected the same thing. "Tennent Brown did it," they told each other. But he was locked up, wasn't he?

Jane asked police, "Could you let me know if Edmonds Tennent Brown IV is still in jail?" When they checked and told her no, she told the police, "You've got him right there."

No one knew he had been released. No one had called Mary Lynn. No *person* had, but a machine had—VINE's automated system had been calling Mary Lynn, but even if she had gotten the message, it would not have helped. The VINE system message was that Tennent was being transferred from the mental facility to the South Carolina Department of Corrections. But that was incorrect. He had been released.

Sergeant Goldstein was convinced Tennent was nearby. "He's one of the lookies—one of the people watching." He was sure Tennent would return soon, so the police packed up and left the house vacant. A stakeout team watched in the shadows of Tradd Street.

Twenty minutes later, Tennent Brown walked down the street with a set of keys in his hand. An officer stopped him, and Tennent identified himself as "Tennent Brown." As soon as Goldstein began to question him, Tennent asked for a lawyer. Goldstein took the keys, and on a hunch "I went up to the front of the house and I was able to open the lock."

When they got to the police station, someone took a good look at Tennent's driver's license. It had been issued that afternoon, with Tennent's name and the Tradd Street address.

Tennent was also wearing Mary Lynn's clothes: a pair of her jeans and her underwear.

NOVEMBER 15, 2003. The letter from VINE arrived in Mary Lynn's mailbox.

A FedEx package was delivered to Mary Lynn's house from a New York boutique. The package contained $429 worth of cross-dressing supplies, including foam breasts, a show girl wig, a beard cover kit, a "how-to-impersonate" tape and some drag queen videos. Tennent had used Mary Lynn's credit card to place the order.

Police found her car. There were several pieces of paper on which Tennent had been practicing Mary Lynn's signature. They also found the most disturbing piece evidence so far—a document Tennent had written while sitting in jail. It was not just the ramblings of an incoherent mind, but also a blueprint for the murder of Mary Lynn and Tennent's plans for his life afterward.

The day that I get out of jail, take care of MLW, take loan out on house.
The next morning place RB and BB on Ice. Then go get two new pairs of

eyeglasses, then go to Highway department and get my new Driver's license in BB's name but with my picture on it. Go to both Bootjack and Walmart to buy new clothes, then go to NEI Truck driver training school to get my Commercial Driver License. Find out how to get a concealed weapons permit for pistol and also how to get a repo license to repossess cars, trucks, and watercraft as well as RVs and mobile homes. After I have obtained the license then find out where I can rent office space with a fenced in yard of about six acres. Go to either Books-A-Million or Barnes + Noble and get the following Magazines as well as books: Soldier of Fortune, Bass, Guns + Ammo, North American Big Game Hunter, American Rifleman, Bowhunting, Wreckmasters, Galls, U.S. Calvary, American Detective, Phoenix Force, Able Team Executioner, Dragons of Pendragon, and anything that has to do with Magic, Witchcraft, mythos, + Mythical creatures, as well as Gunsmithing and weaponsmithing and any that has to do with the aftermath of WW3.

Another letter was discovered in Mary Lynn Witherspoon's car.

Dear Sir,

I would like to bring you up to speed on my current situation. On April 5, 2003 I started a process to change my gender. Ever since I was a small person I have dressed as a female, mostly in private, but I still am sexually inactive. As of this year I thought that now is my opportunity to be complete. This August I was due to move out to Houston for a better paying job as a female considering they are more understanding of my situation and the Company I was going to work for was going to put me up in one of the apartments they own. I would have no problem transferring the probation that I now know that I have. Sir, I would also like to tell you that as a prerequisite for the procedure you have to have both Psychological + psychiatric evaluation and be under a doctors care up until the operation. The surgery itself is an average of $20,000. Please help me.
Edmonds T. Brown IV

Tennent had planned to kill Mary Lynn and take over her life. "He just wanted to be her, and he had to get rid of her to become her," Jackie Olsen said.

NOVEMBER 17, 2003. Mary Lynn Witherspoon's funeral at the French Huguenot Church had so many mourners that police were forced to close down Church Street. Mary Lynn's school cancelled classes for the day.

Mug shot of Tennent Brown. *Courtesy of the South Carolina Department of Corrections.*

Tennent Brown pled guilty to the murder and was sentenced to life imprisonment. During sentencing, he repeatedly tried to express his feelings but, overcome with emotion, he just sobbed and bowed his head toward his shackled feet. "I am extremely sorry," he whispered.

Brown's sentence also included a concurrent life sentence for first-degree burglary and a five-year sentence for possession of a stolen motor vehicle.

Edmonds Tennent Brown III said, "My family and I extend the greatest sympathy to the Witherspoon family and recognize what a tragedy they have experienced. Regarding my son, I wish my attempt during his childhood to discover what his problems were had resulted in an appropriate diagnosis."

MAY 26, 2005. Governor Mark Sanford of South Carolina signed a bill to create Mary Lynn's Law, which requires a mental health exam before bail for anyone arrested on stalking or harassment charges; bans those convicted of a violent offense, stalking, harassment or burglary from pre-trial diversion programs and work-release programs; ends the use of automated recordings to notify victims when a person accused of stalking has been released; and extends temporary restraining orders from six months to a year.

Witherspoon's headstone in the graveyard of the French Huguenot Church, Charleston, South Carolina. *Photo by author.*

DECEMBER 19, 2006. The family of Mary Lynn Witherspoon filed a lawsuit against Charleston County Sheriff's Office, the South Carolina Department of Mental Health, and Department of Corrections. Jackie Olsten stated, "This is not about money. We just felt in our hearts that those people who caused such a gap in the system should be held accountable. This was so avoidable if they had just done their jobs."

Tom Findlay's "Dear John" Letter to Susan Smith

Dear Susan,

I hope you don't mind, but I think clearer when I am typing, so this letter is being written on my computer.

This is a difficult letter for me to write because I know how much you think of me. And I want you to know that I am flattered that you have such a high opinion of me. Susan, I value our friendship very much. You are one of the few people on this earth that I feel I can tell anything. You are intelligent, beautiful, sensitive, understanding, and possess many other wonderful qualities that I and many other men appreciate. You will, without a doubt, make some lucky man a great wife. But unfortunately, it won't be me.

Even though you think we have much in common, we are vastly different. We have been raised in two totally different environments, and therefore, think totally different. That's not to say that I was raised better than you or vice versa, it just means that we come from two different backgrounds.

When I started dating Laura, I knew our backgrounds were going to be a problem. Right before I graduated from Auburn University in 1990, I broke up with a girl (Alison) that I had been dating for over two years. I loved Alison very much and we were very compatible. Unfortunately, we wanted different things out of life. She wanted to get married and have children before the age of 28, and I did not. This conflict spurred our breakup, but we have remained friends through the years. After Alison, I was very hurt. I decided not to fall for anyone again until I was ready to make a long commitment.

For my first two years in Union, I dated very little. In fact, I can count the number of dates I had on one hand. But then Laura came along. We met at Conso, and I fell for her like "a ton of bricks." Things were great at first and remained good for a long time, but I knew deep in my heart that she was not the one for me. People tell me that when you find the person that you will want to spend the rest of your life with…you will know it. Well, even though I fell in love with Laura, I had my doubts about a long and lasting commitment, but I never said anything, and I eventually hurt her very, very deeply. I won't do that again.

Susan, I could really fall for you. You have so many endearing qualities about you, and I think that you are a terrific person. But like I have told you before, there are some things about you that aren't suited for me, and yes, I am speaking about your children. I'm sure that your kids are good kids, but it really wouldn't matter how good they may be…the fact is, I just don't want children. These feelings may change one day, but I doubt it. With all of the crazy, mixed-up things that take place in this world today, I just don't have the desire to bring another life into it. And I don't want to be responsible for anyone else's children, either. But I am very thankful that there are people like you who are not so selfish as I am, and don't mind bearing the responsibility of children. If everyone thought the way that I do, our species would eventually become extinct.

But our differences go far beyond the children issue. We are just two totally different people, and eventually, those differences would cause us to break-up. Because I know myself so well, I am sure of this.

But don't be discouraged. There is someone out there for you. In fact, it's probably someone that you may not know at this time or that you may know, but would never expect. Either way, before you settle down with anyone again, there is something you need to do. Susan, because you got pregnant and married at such an early age, you missed out on much of your youth. I mean, one minute you were a kid, and the next minute you were having kids.

Because I come from a place where everyone had the desire and the money to go to college, having the responsibility of children at such a young age is beyond my comprehension. Anyhow, my advice to you is to wait and be very choosy about your next relationship. I can see this may be a bit difficult for you because you are a bit boy crazy, but as the proverb states "good things come to those who wait." I am not saying you shouldn't go out and have a good time. In fact, I think you should do just that…have a good time and capture some of that youth that you missed out on. But just don't get seriously involved with anyone until you have done the things in life that you want to do, first. Then the rest will fall in place.

Susan, I am not mad at you about what happened this weekend. Actually, I am very thankful. As I told you, I was starting to let my heart warm up to the idea of us going out as more than just friends. But seeing you kiss another man put things back into perspective. I remembered how I hurt Laura, and I won't let that happen again; and therefore, I can't let myself get close to you. We will always be friends, but our relationship will never go beyond that of friendship. And as for your relationship with B. Brown, of course you have to make your own decisions in life, but remember...you have to live with the consequences also. Everyone is held accountable for their actions, and I would hate for people to perceive you as an unreputable person. If you want to catch a nice guy like me one day, you have to act like a nice girl. And you know, nice girls don't sleep with married men. Besides, I want you to feel good about yourself, and I am afraid that if you sleep with B. Brown or any other married man for that matter, you will lose your self-respect. I know I did when we were messing around earlier this year. So please, think about your actions before you do anything you will regret. I care for you, but also care for Susan Brown and I would hate to see anyone get hurt. Susan may say that she wouldn't care [copy illegible] husband had an affair, but you and I know, that is not true.

Anyhow, as I have already told you, you are a very special person. And don't let anyone tell you or make you feel any different. I see so much potential in you, but only you can make it happen. Don't settle for mediocre in life, go for it all and only settle for the best...I do. I haven't told you this, but I am extremely proud of you for going to school. I am a firm believer in higher education, and once you obtain a degree from college, there is no stopping you. And don't let these idiot boys from Union make you feel like you are not capable or slow you down. After you graduate, you will be able to go anywhere you want in this world. And if you ever wanted to get a good job in Charlotte, my father is the right person to know. He and Koni know everyone who is anyone in the business world in Charlotte. And if I can ever help you with anything, don't hesitate to ask.

Well, this letter must come to an end. It is 11:50 p.m. and I am getting very sleepy. But I wanted to write you this letter because you are the one who is always making the effort for me, and I wanted to return the friendship. I've appreciated it when you have dropped me nice little notes, or cards, or the present at Christmas, and it is about time that I start putting a little effort into our friendship. Which reminds me, I thought long and hard about getting you something for your birthday, but I decided not to because I wasn't sure what you might think. Now I am sorry I didn't get you anything, so you can expect something from me at Christmas. But do not buy me anything for Christmas. All I want from you is a nice, sweet card...I'll cherish that more than any store [copy illegible] present.

Again, you will always have my friendship. And your friendship is one that I will always look upon with sincere affection.

Tom

p.s. It's late, so please don't count off for spelling or grammar.

Susan Smith's Confession

When I left my home on Tuesday, Oct. 25, I was very emotionally distraught. I didn't want to live anymore! I felt like things could never get any worse. When I left home, I was going to ride around a little while and then go to my mom's.

As I rode and rode and rode, I felt even more anxiety coming upon me about not wanting to live. I felt I couldn't be a good mom anymore, but I didn't want my children to grow up without a mom. I felt I had to end our lives to protect us from any grief or harm.

I had never felt so lonely and so sad in my entire life. I was in love with someone very much, but he didn't love me and never would. I had a very difficult time accepting that. But I had hurt him very much, and I could see why he could never love me.

When I was at John D. Long Lake, I had never felt so scared and unsure as I did then. I wanted to end my life so bad and was in my car ready to go down that ramp into the water, and I did go part way, but I stopped. I went again and stopped. I then got out of the car and stood by the car a nervous wreck.

Why was I feeling this way? Why was everything so bad in my life? I had no answers to these questions. I dropped to the lowest point when I allowed my children to go down that ramp into the water without me.

I took off running and screaming "Oh God! Oh God, no!" What have I done? Why did you let this happen? I wanted to turn around so bad and go back, but I knew it was too late. I was an absolute mental case! I couldn't believe what I had done.

I love my children with all my (a picture of a heart). That will never change. I have prayed to them for forgiveness and hope that they will find it in their (a picture of a heart) to forgive me. I never meant to hurt them!! I am sorry for what has happened and I know that I need some help. I don't think I will ever be able to forgive myself for what I have done.

My children, Michael and Alex, are with our Heavenly Father now, and I know that they will never be hurt again. As a mom, that means more than words could ever say.

I knew from day one, the truth would prevail, but I was so scared I didn't know what to do. It was very tough emotionally to sit and watch my family hurt like they did. It was time to bring a peace of mind to everyone, including myself.

My children deserve to have the best, and now they will. I broke down on Thursday, Nov. 3, and told Sheriff Howard Wells the truth. It wasn't easy, but after the truth was out, I felt like the world was lifted off my shoulders.

I know now that it is going to be a tough and long road ahead of me. At this very moment, I don't feel I will be able to handle what's coming, but I have prayed to God that he give me the strength to survive each day and to face those times and situations in my life that will be extremely painful. I have put my total faith in God, and he will take care of me.

Susan V. Smith
11/3/94 5:05 p.m.

The confession was signed by a FBI agent and a State Law Enforcement Division agent.

Bibliography

Newspapers, Magazines and Other Sources

Callahan, Karen. "Interview with Katherine Stinney Robinson." Corporation for Public Broadcasting.

———. "Interview with Lorraine Binnicker Bailey." Corporation for Public Broadcasting.

Charleston *Evening Post.* July 1911.

Charleston *News and Courier.* June–July 1910.

———. October 1910.

———. April 18, 1974.

———. November 2003.

Dateline, NBC, "Fatal Attraction." November 8, 2006.

Newman, H.L. Deputy. "Written statement to Clarendon County Court," 1944.

Official Detective Stories Magazine. New York: TD Publishing Corp., April 1942.

Rowe, Mrs. Ernest. "Alcolu Negro Boy to Die for Slaying Girl." *State*, April 25, 1944.

Schoen, Elin. "Does This Woman Deserve To Die?" *Village Voice,* June 5, 1984.

State, March 26, April 25, and June 17, 1944.

State v. Tucker, 464 S.E.2d 105 (S.C. 1995) (Mellon Murder Direct Appeal).

Turnipseed, Tom. "Continuing Saga of Sex, Murder & Racism: Susan Smith Is Still Scheming In Prison." *Common Dreams News Center*, September 14, 2000.

Books and Manuscripts

Bass, Jack, and Marilyn Robinson. *Ol' Strom: An Unauthorized Biography of Strom Thurmond*. Columbia: University of South Carolina Press, 2003.

————. *Strom: The Complicated Personal and Political Life of Strom Thurmond*. New York: Public Affairs Books, 2005.

Beacham, Frank. *Whitewash: A Southern Journey through Music, Mayhem and Murder*. New York: Booklocker.com, Inc., 2002

Crooks, D.J., Jr. *The Trial of Daniel Duncan*. Charleston County Public Library, South Carolina Room Collection, 1999.

Dorn, T. Felder. *The Guns of Meeting Street: A Southern Tragedy*. Columbia: University of South Carolina Press, 2001.

Eftimiades, Maria. *Sins of the Mother*. New York: St. Martin's Paperbacks, 1995.

Henderson, Gary. *Nine Days in Union: The Search for Alex and Michael Smith*. Spartanburg, SC: Honoribus Press, 1995.

Jones, Ann. *Women Who Kill*. Boston: Beacon Press, 1996.

Jones, Lewis Pinckney. *Stormy Petrel: N.G. Gonzales and His State*. Columbia: South Carolina Tricentennial Commission, University of South Carolina Press, 1973.

Jones, Mark R. *Wicked Charleston, Volume 2: Prostitutes, Politics and Prohibition.* Charleston, SC: The History Press, 2006.

Moore, John Hammond. *Carnival of Blood: Dueling, Lynching and Murder in South Carolina 1880–1920.* Columbia: University of South Carolina Press, 2006.

Ravenel, Beatrice St. J., ed. *Charleston Murders.* New York: Duell, Sloan & Pierce, 1947.

Rekers, George. *Susan Smith: Victim or Murderer.* Lakewood, CO: Glenbridge Publishing, Ltd., 1996.

Rhyne, Nancy. *Murder in the Carolinas.* Greensboro, NC: Avisson Press, Inc., 1998.

Simkins, Francis Butler. *Pitchfork Ben Tillman: South Carolinian.* Baton Rouge, LA, 1944.

Smith, David, with Carol Calef. *Beyond All Reason: My Life with Susan Smith.* New York: Kensington Books, 1995.

Wilkins, Robert. *Death: A History of Man's Obsessions and Fears.* New York: Barnes & Noble Books, 1996.

About the Author

Mark R. Jones is a historian, author, tour guide and speaker. During an average year, Mark conducts tours and speaks in front of more than six thousand people.

Mark is the author of two bestselling books on Charleston history: *Wicked Charleston: The Dark Side of the Holy City* and *Wicked Charleston, Volume 2: Prostitutes, Politics and Prohibition.* His next project is a collection on South Carolina serial killers called *Palmetto Predators: Monsters Among Us.*

As a licensed city of Charleston tour guide, Mark is co-owner of Black Cat Tours, which specializes in nighttime walking tours, including the Wicked Walk, the only tour based on the *Wicked Charleston* books. He also drives carriages for Palmetto Carriage Works.

Mark believes there are two versions of Southern history: the water-colored version of flowers and quaint streets, where all the women were ladies and all the men were gentle, and the sepia-toned version of hard drinkers, scoundrels, wayward ministers, prostitutes and murderers. Even though the Charleston tourism industry works hard at selling the former, Mark prefers to give tours and write books about the latter, as they are more interesting than romantic caricatures.

He lives in Charleston with fellow tour guide and romance novelist Rebel Sinclair. Their household includes a dog named Megan, a black cat named Edgar Allan Poe and a noose in the hallway. Visit Mark online at www. blackcattours.com and www.wickedcharleston.net.

Visit us at
www.historypress.net